GOVERNMENT SUBSIDY TO INDUSTRY

by Jeffrey H. Hacker

Franklin Watts
New York I London I
Toronto I Sydney I 1982
An Impact Book

Photographs courtesy of Wide World Photos: p. 2;
United Press International Photo: pp. 18, 32, 52.

Cartoons courtesy of Rothco Cartoons: (Rosen—
Albany Times Union, N.Y.) p. 14; (Pletcher—
Times/Picayune—States/Item, New Orleans) p.
46; (Al Liederman, Long Island Press, N.Y.) p.
58; (Taylor—Albuquerque, N. Mex.) p. 78.

Library of Congress Cataloging in Publication Data

Hacker, Jeffrey H.
Government subsidy to industry

(An Impact book)
Bibliography: p.
Includes index.

Summary: Examines the various forms of government
subsidies to industry and agriculture, traces the development of our subsidized economy, and discusses the
related growth of government regulations and lobbying.
1. Subsidies—United States—Juvenile literature
[1. Subsidies] I. Title

HD3646.U6H32 1982   338.973′02   82-8393
ISBN 0-531-04487-4   AACR2

Contents

To my parents

CHAPTER 1

Taking Care of Business

On July 31, 1979, John J. Riccardo, the chairman and chief executive officer of Chrysler Corporation, faced an auditorium full of reporters at company headquarters in Highland Park, Michigan. There had been rumors of an important development at the financially-troubled automobile manufacturer, but few of the journalists at that press conference could have predicted what Riccardo was about to announce.

Chrysler—the third largest car manufacturer in the United States and the nation's tenth biggest corporation overall—had lost a whopping $207.1 million in the second quarter of the year. It was the largest three-month loss in the history of the company, and the future looked even worse. But that was not the shocker.

"We have taken all the prudent steps that could be taken to make our way," said Chairman Riccardo. There was nothing left to do but look for help. But from whom? The government. Chrysler was asking the United States government for $1 billion in cash to save it from going out of business. Company officials had already visited Wash-

Chrysler's chairman, John J. Riccardo, announcing his request for $1 billion from the government to save the nation's third largest auto manufacturer.

ington to appeal to Congress and the Carter administration for a special cash advance against future tax deductions.

Riccardo's announcement set off a vigorous national debate. In the media, in financial and business circles, in government offices and hearing rooms, and in private gatherings across the country, the question was asked: Should the government save Chrysler? Those favoring the emergency funding, or bailout, were concerned about the hundreds of thousands of workers who would lose their jobs if Chrysler folded. Those opposing the bailout insisted that Uncle Sam could not play the role of "rich uncle" to every American corporation in financial trouble.

Yet, with all the arguing and all the debating, the fact remained that Chrysler was only a small part of the story. Then—and now—many private companies in a wide range of industries receive vital financial assistance from the federal government. From giant steel manufacturers, to dairy farms, to "mom and pop" grocery stores, American businesses of every size and type depend on help from their rich uncle.

The federal government has always lent a helping hand to private enterprise. Since the earliest days of the republic, Washington has done its best to keep certain businesses running. As the years went by, it bestowed greater and greater benefits on the private sector. The depression of the 1930s saw an especially dramatic increase in the economic role of government. In the decades since, programs have been created to help virtually every major industry in the United States—transportation, housing, agriculture, shipping, scientific research, and even the arts. Today, a large part of the government's overall yearly budget is set aside for *subsidies* to private industry.

The term *subsidy* is hard to define. Government assistance is provided in so many different forms, for so many different purposes, that it is not always clear which should be called subsidies. To avoid confusion, the term will be used in this book for *all* the benefits—both direct and indirect—provided by the federal government to assist private business and industry.

Because of the enormous variety of support programs sponsored by the federal government, it is also quite difficult to know exactly how much money is spent on industrial and agricultural subsidies. It would not be an exaggeration, however, to estimate a total expenditure of hundreds of billions of dollars a year.

The growth of the subsidized economy and the expansion of federal authority occurred gradually over a long period of time, with little pause for serious debate. In recent years, however, two events in particular have aroused public concern over the trend. One was Chrysler's plea for emergency financial aid. The other was the election of Ronald Reagan as president. The Chrysler bailout request posed the question of how far the government should go to protect an individual company. President Reagan posed a more direct challenge to American economic trends of the previous fifty years. He called for a massive reduction in government spending, the elimination or cutting back of countless federal service and aid programs, and a squelching of the idea—which he perceived as having evolved over several decades—that Washington could provide all things for all people.

What purposes do government subsidies serve? Have they gotten out of hand? Are they necessary at all? What are the alternatives? Should the federal government interfere in private business?

On one hand, subsidies protect businesses and industries from financial disaster. As in the case of Chrysler, they often keep many thousands of workers from losing their jobs. They insure farmers against natural disasters, such as droughts, floods, and storms. They give a boost to owners of small businesses who would otherwise be gobbled up by competition from giant companies. Finally, and perhaps most importantly, they help keep the nation's economy running smoothly. They help make sure that enough goods are produced and enough services provided. Without government help, private firms would never engage in certain activities—such as building highways, developing a space program, and carrying out basic scientific and industrial research—that are sorely needed if the society is to prosper.

On the other hand, there is a basic unfairness built into the subsidized economy. The government purposely helps out certain groups at the expense of others. Different industries receive different kinds of aid; some companies get more than others. In addition this approach offends a very basic American principle: a free enterprise economy in which businesses operate without government interference. The capitalist system becomes diluted when the government steps into the private sector. There is less competition. In the debate over Chrysler, for example, a basic question was whether granting the bailout money would be unfair to Chrysler's competitors. The preservation of free-enterprise capitalism is not only a question of fairness to individual companies, but also, as will be seen in a later chapter, one of economic efficiency for the whole country.

The financial assistance doled out by Washington is largely paid for by taxpayers. Where should the government draw the line? How much can it afford to give out before the burden becomes too heavy? How many programs can it manage and support before losing control? How much authority can it assume before it gets too powerful?

These issues go to the very heart of the American way of life. The institution of federal subsidies, the status of Chrysler (and other companies that might fall into a similar situation), the economic policies of President Reagan, and the power of the federal government all affect our daily lives in very significant ways. The debates sometimes seem highly technical, and the arguments are often based on complicated economic theories. But, as this book will show, subsidies to industry and agriculture affect our homes, food, medical care, job security, transportation, and other fundamental needs. In the everyday life of the student, subsidies affect the cost of filling up the gas tank, buying clothes, finding a part-time job, the quality of education, and even the cost of entertainment. The issue is vital to our security, well-being, and quality of life, now and in the future. It is one worth thinking about.

As a basic introduction to the subject, this book describes how subsidies work, who gets them, how they have grown, what purposes they serve, and why the government provides them. The aim throughout is to stimulate debate in the mind of the reader. There are many considerations on both sides of this increasingly controversial issue. The answers are never clear-cut. Sometimes the questions themselves are subtle and hard to pick out. The most important consideration, however, should always be how *people* will be affected.

Chrysler's bailout request in 1979 tested the limits of U.S. government generosity. The debate that followed covered many of the arguments for and against federal participation in the private sector. Although the issue of government subsidies touches virtually every type of American business and industry, a closer look at the Chrysler controversy is a good place to start.

CHAPTER 2

Chrysler– An Extreme Case

Ten days after John Riccardo's press conference, the Carter administration made a formal response to Chrysler's SOS. Secretary of the Treasury G. William Miller called his own news conference to issue a statement. "In general," he said, "governmental financial assistance to private companies is neither desirable nor appropriate." But, he went on, "there is a public interest in sustaining the jobs and productive capability represented by the Chrysler facilities and in maintaining a strong and competitive national automotive industry." The White House would not authorize cash subsidies, as Riccardo had requested, but it would consider a proposal for loan guarantees. In other words, the government was promising to repay lending institutions if Chrysler could not meet its obligations.

Miller's response was both encouraging for Chrysler and discouraging for any other company that might request money in the future. Although the administration would try to work something out for Chrysler, it would not come to the rescue of every failing corporation in the country. One staff member in the Carter White House summed up the attitude: "I think we see Chrysler as a special situation."

The company's financial problems did create a unique set of possibilities. Chrysler was the largest U.S. corporation ever to ask the government for emergency financial aid. If its request were granted, the government would be taking on the biggest federal bailout of a private company in U.S. history. If the plea were rejected, Chrysler would likely become the largest U.S. corporation ever to go bankrupt.

The consequences of Chrysler closing its doors were potentially disastrous. Literally hundreds of thousands of workers would lose their jobs. The nation was already facing economic difficulties, and the collapse of an industrial giant might have serious, far-reaching effects. In short, could the government afford *not* to save Chrysler?

On the other hand, what if the government's initial help were not enough? Would it then be committed to even greater outlays? Was it fair to save Chrysler but nobody else? Would granting aid to Chrysler give it an unfair advantage over other car manufacturers? Wouldn't the assistance to Chrysler amount to a reward for its failures?

In pleading their case to Congress over the next several months, Chrysler officials emphasized the fact that many other companies depend on help from their rich Uncle Sam. In light of the vast federal outlay for subsidy programs, and in light of the wide variety of industries that receive some type of benefit from the government, Chrysler's situation was not completely unique. Because it was the largest company ever to ask for so much direct aid, it was—as the Carter administration saw it—a "special case." However, in light of the strong tradition of U.S. government largess, it might be more accurate to call Chrysler an *extreme* case.

Chairman Riccardo's call for help, therefore, is usefully understood as the next step in, perhaps the culmination of, the steady growth of a subsidized economy. In deciding

[8]

whether to rescue Chrysler—and if so, how—Congress and the Carter administration had to analyze not only the company's financial predicament and who was to blame, but also the entire automobile industry, its importance in the nation's economy, and how it would be affected.

Ups and Downs

Since its birth in the late 1800s, automobile manufacturing has grown to be one of the great industries of the world. It is vital to the economies of the major industrial powers, especially the United States. Competition among the "Big Three" American manufacturers (General Motors, Ford, and Chrysler) made the United States the world's leading producer of motor vehicles for more than eight decades. Then, in 1980, the United States lost that lead. Supporters of the Chrysler bailout felt that a spirit of healthy competition among the Big Three had to be restored. Indeed, the rise and fall of the Chrysler Corporation had closely paralleled the ups and downs of the entire U.S. automobile industry.

When Henry Ford's moving assembly line became fully operational in 1913, the price of a commercially manufactured automobile came within reach of the general public. America began its love affair with anything on four wheels. In the 1920s, the shape of the nation's automobile industry emerged clearly. General Motors (GM) and Ford dominated the market, with the Chrysler Corporation a distant fifth. Chrysler was formed in 1925, after Walter P Chrysler, a former railway machinist from Kansas and ex-employee of GM, had reorganized the bankrupt Maxwell Motor Company. The Chrysler Corporation became a major contributor to the industry when it acquired the Dodge firm in 1928 and broke into the low-priced market with the Plymouth.

By developing regional assembly lines and a network of

local dealerships, the Big Three—GM, Ford, and Chrysler—took control of the industry. By 1929, they held three-quarters of the U.S. market. GM was the most innovative and successful of the auto manufacturers, offering cars in a variety of colors and introducing new models every year. It was by following these innovations that Chrysler remained competitive. Such competition among the Big Three worked magic on sales, and total U.S. production rose to 5 million in 1929.

The Great Depression and challenges from organized labor brought a significant decline in the 1930s, but the setback was only temporary. After World War II, the industry grew steadily, year in and year out. The United States preserved its lead in world motor vehicle production despite rapid growth by foreign manufacturers. The nation's output reached a peak of 13 million in 1978.

It was during the 1970s, however, that the American car industry was challenged by several external factors. The Organization of Petroleum Exporting Countries (OPEC), representing the world's major oil producers, drastically increased the price of crude oil and cut back on production. The United States, which relies heavily on imported oil, faced serious shortages. The price of a gallon of gas rose by several hundred percent in the second half of the decade, and the American consumer looked toward smaller, more fuel-efficient cars. The industry was not prepared, and its output declined substantially.

At the same time, Japanese auto manufacturers were flourishing. Between 1957 and 1980, the total Japanese output of motor vehicles increased from 100,000 to 11 million per year. In 1980, Japan surpassed the United States to become the world's leading producer. Its cars were small and highly fuel-efficient, which met the needs of the American consumer. That year, U.S. auto manufacturers lost more than a quarter of their market to foreign imports. The Big Three and other car manufacturers were awash in red ink.

"A Strategic National Industry"

Congress considered a variety of ways to provide relief for the struggling U.S. auto industry. One way was to limit imports of Japanese cars. That would force American consumers to buy more U.S.-made and fewer Japanese-made cars. But because Japan is a close ally, U.S. lawmakers were reluctant to deal so harsh a blow to its foreign trade. Establishing import quotas was a sticky matter, and no legislation was forthcoming from Congress in 1980. In June of that year, however, the Senate and House of Representatives adopted a resolution calling for a revitalization of the industry. By overwhelming majorities, both houses agreed that

> the American automobile and truck industry is a strategic national industry that is essential to the economic stability and national security of the the United States.

Although the resolution did not call for any specific corrective measures, it did emphasize that a vital national interest would be served by preserving, if not strengthening, the U.S. automotive industry. On that point there was little disagreement.

The business of making cars employs more workers than any other U.S. manufacturing industry. Nearly one of every twenty manufacturing jobs in the country is related to motor vehicle production; more than 1 million people are employed in the actual manufacturing of motor vehicles, parts, and equipment. Including distribution and sales, maintenance and service, and commercial use, some 15 mil-

[11]

lion people rely on the industry for their income. In short, the auto industry and related fields employ a sizeable portion of the entire U.S. labor force—about one-fifth.

Moreover, the performance of the Big Three and other manufacturers affects a whole range of "ancillary," or indirectly related, industries. These include steel, iron, aluminum, copper, rubber, gasoline, oil, and others. In 1980, the production of motor vehicles in the United States consumed nearly 25 percent of the nation's steel output, 54 percent of iron, 60 percent of synthetic rubber, and 17 percent of aluminum. The manufacture of cars, trucks, and buses is crucial to the survival of these major industries. Any significant decline in motor vehicle production is a severe blow to each of them.

Chrysler Runs Out of Gas

Most business and economic analysts agreed that Chrysler's problems were directly related to the external forces impinging on the entire U.S. automobile industry. But other car manufacturers faced the same set of circumstances and emerged, if not unscathed, at least less seriously wounded than Chrysler. There was no doubt that decisions made inside the company's executive offices contributed to Chrysler's difficulties. In the 1960s, when the seeds of change were sown in the U.S. automobile market, Chrysler was expanding its foreign operations at the expense of its U.S. factories. During the national economic slowdown of 1974, Chrysler's engineering and design staffs were cut back, which also delayed the emergence of small, fuel-efficient cars. Then, when the real change came, the company still misread the market and in 1976 decided not to build a new plant for small (four-cylinder) engines. In short, it expected Americans to return to buying larger cars when the gasoline crisis was over. When instead they bought high-mileage compacts and subcompacts—many of them imports—Chrysler's fate was sealed.

The company quickly amassed a large inventory of unsold vehicles. By August 1979, the total reached about 80,000—worth $700 million. Most of them were big cars. In the manufacturing year ending August 1979, production dropped by about 117,000 vehicles from the previous year.

Financial losses went hand in hand. The company finished out 1978 with a net loss of $204.6 million, and that was only the beginning. The red ink got darker by $53.8 million in the first quarter of 1978, followed by a record $207.1 million loss in the second quarter. That was when Riccardo turned to the government. As it turned out, the $1 billion he asked for would not have offset the company's losses for 1979 alone. At the end of the fourth quarter, the net loss for 1979 stood at $1.1 billion. Even with a federal bailout, the losses were expected to continue into 1980. Without one, there was simply no way to turn the tide.

The Costs of Bankruptcy
Although Chairman Riccardo said from the start that Chrysler would not go bankrupt, without cash the once-great auto manufacturer simply could not continue producing cars, much less reverse its enormous deficit. That prospect had Congress and the Carter administration deeply concerned. Senator Russell B. Long of Louisiana, the influential chairman of the Senate Finance Committee, declared that "letting that company fold would cost us a lot of revenue, a lot of jobs."

A study by the Congressional Budget Office predicted that if Chrysler went under there would be an immediate loss of up to 500,000 jobs. Chrysler employees would represent only about 130,000 of these; the rest would come

"BUDDY, CAN YOU SPARE A BILLION?"

This cartoon shows Chrysler's president, Lee A. Iacocca, as a beggar, reduced to selling pencils while he strangles on the red tape of government regulations that Chrysler officials blamed for the company's financial troubles.

from suppliers and clients who depended on the company. Permanent job loss, the study concluded, would total 200,000 to 300,000. With national unemployment already at a high level, such losses would put an enormous burden on federal welfare, unemployment compensation, and pension guarantee programs. The losses would occur primarily in the seven states in which the U.S. auto industry is centered—Michigan, Ohio, Pennsylvania, Illinois, Indiana, Missouri, and Delaware. Especially hard hit would be older, struggling cities. In Detroit, for example, where Chrysler is the single largest employer, a collapse might mean an increase in unemployment of up to 50 percent. Blacks would bear most of the hardship.

There were, to be fair, a good many economists who argued that the effects of Chrysler's demise would not be so severe. Alan Greenspan, the chairman of the President's Council of Economic Advisers under Gerald Ford, maintained that other companies would buy up Chrysler's assets, that competitors would hire its unemployed workers, and that the nation's undiminished demand for automobiles would be met. Senator William Proxmire of Wisconsin, Chairman of the Senate Banking Committee, agreed. Writing in an article in *The New York Times Magazine*, he said: "The number of cars bought by the American public will not diminish simply because Chrysler goes into bankruptcy. The other two automobile companies, moving in to fill the void, will hire many Chrysler employees." The prediction of a 500,000 job loss was, according to Proxmire, "patently ridiculous."

Even so, the prospect of the other two major producers (GM and Ford) picking up Chrysler's lost market raised another important issue: competition. If Chrysler went out of business, some argued, the industry would no longer be competitive. GM already held 60 percent of the U.S. market. Ralph Nader, the well-known advocate of consumer

[15]

rights, announced that if GM increased its share any more, he would call for antitrust proceedings against the company to investigate the possibility of monopolistic practices. The U.S. Treasury Department also saw a problem: if there were only two American companies producing a full line of cars, the door would be open for even greater foreign intrusion. As will be seen in later chapters, however, the issue of marketplace competition is both complicated and controversial. Indeed, there were many who believed that the effects on competition would be neither far-reaching nor undesirable.

Finally, supporters of a bailout maintained that a collapse by Chrysler would be a blow to the nation's defenses. Although it had always relied on car manufacturing for most of its profits, Chrysler was also a major supplier of tanks to the army.

Who's to Blame?
While even the Chrysler management could not deny that the company's problems were partly of its own making, they did insist that forces beyond their control were more directly responsible. In addition to the gasoline crisis and the economic slowdown, government regulation was said to be a major cause. In his plea for help, Chairman Riccardo laid much of the blame for Chrysler's predicament on the high cost of meeting federal air-pollution, safety, and fuel-efficiency standards. In the previous five years, the company claimed to have spent $8.6 billion to comply with these increasingly tough regulations. The problem, said Riccardo, was not only the actual cost of compliance, but the fact that the regulations placed an unfair burden on smaller manufacturers. In order to meet the federal requirements, Chrysler had to spend as much as GM to develop the necessary technology. But because GM produced many more vehicles, Chrysler was at a disadvantage. The average cost

of improving each vehicle at Chrysler was $620, or almost twice as much as GM's cost of $340. Without the added expense, Riccardo maintained, Chrysler would have been better able to develop and produce the small, fuel-efficient cars the public wanted to buy.

Justifiably or not, Riccardo argued that Chrysler had been victimized by the government. "I believe," he said, "the government will take action to correct some of the problems that have been caused by government regulation."

The government, for its part, did not react as if it *owed* Chrysler anything. Relief from federal emission requirements never did come, and financial help—in the form of loan guarantees rather than an outright cash advance—was nearly five months in the making. The aid package, which required special legislation by Congress and approval by the president, emerged out of a variety of proposals by Chrysler, the Treasury Department, and members of both houses of Congress.

To the Rescue
After Treasury Secretary Miller rejected Riccardo's first plea for a cash tax advance, Chrysler officials went back to the drawing board to come up with a suitable loan guarantee proposal. Also, to stimulate sales, bolster the corporate image, and otherwise strengthen its position, the company hired a new advertising agency, offered rebates on the purchase of new cars, reduced its workforce, and cut executive salaries.

On September 15, Chrysler submitted to the Carter administration a formal request for $1.2 billion in federal loan guarantees. Again Secretary Miller turned the company down. The figure was "way out of line," he said. In order to be considered, the request "would have to be well below $1 billion." Two days later, Chrysler Chairman Riccardo

[17]

Lee Iacocca makes a gracious bow to President Carter following Carter's signing of the bill granting Chrysler $1.5 billion in federal loan guarantees.

announced suddenly that he was seeking immediate early retirement because of poor health and the belief that his association with the company's troubles might be hurting its chances of winning government aid. Lee A. Iacocca, Chrysler's president and former president of Ford, was named as Riccardo's successor. The new leadership immediately went about the business of convincing Washington to provide help.

Congress and the Treasury Department, meanwhile, had also been hard at work figuring out ways to solve Chrysler's problems. Among the suggestions were tax breaks, state aid, loans from other federal agencies, easing of regulation requirements, and even employee ownership of the company.

Finally, on November 1, the Carter administration said yes to Chrysler and submitted a bill to Congress for aid to the car manufacturer. Oddly, the bill called for $1.5 billion in loan guarantees, a figure considerably higher than the one that had been rejected six weeks before. Secretary Miller said that the administration had had "a change of outlook" regarding the auto industry and its role in the national economy.

Buoyed by an intensive lobbying campaign, the proposed legislation was well-received in both houses of Congress. There was some opposition, and minor changes were made in the bill. But on December 21, 1979, the House and Senate gave final approval to the biggest bailout in the history of the U.S. government. It was signed into law on January 7, 1980, by President Jimmy Carter. The aid plan would provide Chrysler with $1.5 billion in federal backing if the company could raise $2 billion on its own. The subsidy would be administered by a board made up of three voting members—the Secretary of the Treasury, the Chairman of the Federal Reserve Board, and the Comptroller of the Currency.

[19]

As President Carter made clear in his remarks at the bill-signing ceremony, the government came to the aid of Chrysler simply because it was deemed in the national interest:

> *This legislation, the Chrysler Corporation Loan Guarantee Act of 1979, is extremely important not only for Chrysler and its employees, its dealers, its suppliers, not only important for Detroit but for all the people in our country and, I think, almost every community. . . .*
>
> *It's important to have Chrysler preserved as a viable competitive entity, not only to protect jobs involved but to protect the competitive nature of the American automobile manufacturing industry in its competition with foreign suppliers and in the provision of good products at a competitive price for the American consumer.*

The Chrysler debate was over, but with a presidential campaign and the election of Ronald Reagan just around the corner, the issue of government subsidies and the role of the federal government was by no means dead.

CHAPTER 3

The Heart
of the Matter

Congress and the Carter administration were taking a considerable risk in providing financial assistance to Chrysler. They had closely scrutinized the company's prospects for the future. They had carefully weighed the alternatives to a federal bailout. They had attached strict conditions and stipulations to the final agreement. Above all, they had determined that saving Chrysler was important for the economic well-being of the nation. But, whenever the federal government steps into the private sector to help a business or industry—whether it is on the brink of bankruptcy or financially sound—something else is at stake.

Thomas A. Murphy, the chairman of General Motors, was among many people who believed that the granting of special emergency aid to Chrysler would seriously threaten some fundamental American principles. The request for help by his competitor, said Murphy, "presents a basic challenge to the philosophy of America." While the Chrysler bailout was not totally without precedent, it did add a new chapter to the continuing story of government expansion. Seen as the next step in the evolution of a subsidized

[21]

economy, it posed vital questions regarding the accumulated economic effects of increasing government activity. Even though saving Chrysler was deemed to be in the national interest, it was the culmination of a trend toward government control that many citizens regarded, and still regard, as dangerous.

One of those citizens was a former governor of California, Ronald Reagan. Campaigning on a platform of fiscal restraint and a more limited role for the federal government, Reagan won the Republican Party nomination for president and easily defeated Jimmy Carter in the November 1980 election. In his inaugural address on January 20, 1981, President Reagan blamed the nation's "economic affliction" on that trend:

> *It is no coincidence that our present problems parallel and are proportionate to the intervention and intrusion in our lives that result from unnecessary and excessive growth of government.*

To resolve those problems, proclaimed Reagan, "it is my intention to curb the size and influence of the federal establishment."

The new administration would take three major steps to reduce the size of government and cure the economy: 1) limit government spending; 2) reduce taxes; and 3) lift many of the controls and regulations established by federal agencies.

The proposed cuts in government spending raised a storm of controversy. Now in jeopardy were scores of personal benefit and industrial subsidy programs that had been born in the past several decades. Food stamps, medical care, unemployment insurance, and other social programs would be cut back substantially. In the area of business and industry, aid would be reduced for everything from transportation and commerce, to farming, energy, and housing. Reagan was calling for a return to the principles of free enterprise, individual initiative, and limited government influence. The federal authority would lift many of its regulations, lighten the tax burden, and otherwise loosen its grip on agriculture and industry. This would mean more in the way of direct competition but less in the way of subsidies.

The United States has long been recognized as the foremost capitalist nation in the world. The basic principles of that system were first articulated by a Scottish professor, Adam Smith, in the eighteenth century. His book *The Wealth of Nations* (1776) set out the classical arguments for a system based on economic freedom. A central principle of Smith's philosophy was the so-called invisible hand. According to that doctrine, individuals will pursue—as if led by an invisible hand—the best interests of society, if government does not interfere. Members of a society know what is best for them. If they are not restricted by government, they will be motivated to produce the goods and services the public desires.

The opposite extreme of Adam Smith's free-enterprise system is one in which the state owns and controls every business and industry. Such an arrangement is most closely represented in today's world by the Communist systems of the Soviet Union and China. However, the differences between American capitalism and Soviet or Chinese communism are becoming less extreme. In recent years, the Soviets and Chinese have been turning toward more private ownership and free enterprise in some industries. In the United States, meanwhile, the trend for several decades has been toward greater government involvement. The growth of federal subsidies has meant a gradual shift in the direction of a state-controlled economy. As a result, the Chrysler bailout, representing yet another step in that direction, touched on some highly-charged issues. In attempting to pull back the federal government, President Reagan was also taking a strong ideological position against that shift in direction. His economic policies were applauded by conservatives and resisted by liberals.

In the debate over Chrysler, one of the strongest voices opposing a bailout was that of a young Republican congressman from Michigan, David Stockman. Despite intense pressure from fellow Michigan representatives, Stockman refused to go along with any assistance program even though a collapse by the auto manufacturer posed a serious economic threat to his home state. In fact, Stockman helped circulate a letter on Capitol Hill which opposed a bailout on principle alone: the government simply should not interfere in private business. "There are no circumstances," said one of Stockman's aides, "in which federal aid would be appropriate."

Although Stockman was overruled on the Chrysler issue, his conservative voice would be heard again, this time even louder. A campaign supporter of Ronald Reagan, Stockman was named director of the Office of Management and Budget in the new administration. It was his job to "carve away the fat" in the federal budget. On March 10, 1981, President Reagan formally submitted to Congress his budget proposal for fiscal—or financial—year 1982; it called for $48.6 billion in spending cuts. In a televised interview a few weeks earlier, Stockman summed up the administration's thinking: "We felt government had grown excessively, that it was doing things it shouldn't be doing, that it was funding activities that weren't appropriate."

Exactly what is "appropriate" government activity? The question is a highly philosophical one that has occupied the human mind for many centuries. Any thorough answer implies basic assumptions about society and human nature. Differences of opinion have been the cause of wars, revolutions, and social upheavals everywhere. It is this weighty issue, with all its implications and all its subtleties, that lies at the heart of the debate over government subsidies.

At the heart of the question of "appropriate" government activity, however, lies an even more basic concern: human welfare. Certainly the government must always seek to do what is in the best interest of the people—not special interest groups or a particular segment of the population, but the society as a whole. But what is in the best interest of society as a whole?

The answers are never obvious, and the Chrysler dilemma was a perfect case in point. The grim prospect for thousands of workers was that they would lose their jobs if the company folded. Moreover, the rest of the nation would be hurt because of the resulting decline in overall industrial production, foreign trading power, and employment. The government, therefore, decided that saving Chrysler was in the best interest of the nation as a whole. Opponents of the bailout, on the other hand, also argued on behalf of the nation as a whole. They felt that a bailout would serve too narrow a segment of the population. They felt that every individual citizen would be better served *in the long term* if we maintain a free-enterprise system and let businesses take care of themselves.

With regard to the government's many ongoing industrial subsidy programs—those designed for day-to-day support rather than financial emergencies—the best interests of the public are even less clear. Those who favor a strong central government and more federal participation insist that subsidy programs are vital to essential industries, help control the economy, support small businesses, keep farmers productive, and serve the good of the people in other important ways.

[25]

Those who favor less government intervention, meanwhile, contend that federal subsidies have grown too costly and actually inhibit the production of goods needed by the public. Government itself has grown too powerful, they say. It is time for government "to get off the backs" of the people.

The central question today is this: At what point does the expansion of government activity undermine economic growth in a pure free-enterprise system? In other words, has the subsidized economy gotten out of hand? Has the good of the people been lost in the shuffle?

If so, when and how?

CHAPTER 4

The Mixing of the Economy

On January 31, 1829—one hundred and fifty years before Chrysler's Chairman John Riccardo made his plea to the government—Martin Van Buren, who was then the governor of New York, sent a letter to the president of the United States, Andrew Jackson. In his letter, Van Buren informed the president that the nation's canal system was in serious danger and that the government should step in to help.

> The canal system of this country is being threatened by the spread of a new form of transportation known as "railroads." The federal government must preserve the canals for the following reasons:
>
> One. If canal boats are supplanted by "railroads" serious unemployment will result. . . .
>
> Two. Boat builders would suffer and tow-line and harness makers would be left destitute. . . .
>
> Three. Canal boats are absolutely essential to the defense of the United States. . . .

> *For the above-mentioned reasons the government should create an Interstate Commerce Commission to protect the American people from the evil of "railroads" and to preserve canals for posterity.*
>
> *As you may well know, Mr. President, "railroad" carriages are pulled at the enormous speed of 15 miles per hour by "engines" which, in addition to endangering life and limb of passengers, roar and snort their way through the countryside, setting fire to crops, scaring livestock, and frightening women and children. The Almighty certainly never intended that people should travel at such breakneck speed.*

Although the Interstate Commerce Commission as envisioned by Governor Van Buren did not immediately come into existence, an agency was established in 1887 for the purpose of protecting shippers from the competition of railroads. An undeniable truth in our nation's history is that the federal government has never been able to keep entirely out of the affairs of the private sector. Threatened businesses have looked to Washington for help even since the days when 15 miles per hour was considered "breakneck speed."

Since that time, federal support for private enterprise has benefited an ever-growing number of industries. It has been offered in an enormous variety of new forms, and it has increased in cost to many billions of dollars per year. Yet, as shown in chapter 2, the U.S. economy is still regarded as fundamentally capitalist, with roots in the classical free-enterprise principles of Adam Smith. There is more private ownership, more direct competition among businesses, and less government interference than in almost any other country in the world.

To reflect the conflicting strains in our economic history—a strong tradition of free enterprise but extensive federal involvement—the U.S. economy is commonly described as a *mixed economy.* It is controlled by both private and public institutions.[1] It is still based on private ownership, but the government plays an important role. The expansion of government influence has been a long process, which can be called "the mixing of the economy."

Beginnings

In the early days of the republic, the federal government realized that it would have to play an important role in the development of the nation's economy. Its help was felt in many areas, including the settlement of public land; the construction of roads; aid for the building of canals, dams, and irrigation projects; the postal service; and numerous others.

Even with all its help, the government felt that it should avoid interfering with private enterprise as much as possible. Too much federal control would not only contradict the principles of the new republic, but it would also jeopardize the stability and growth of the economy. In the 1800s, the government did assist greatly in the development of a national railroad network and certain other areas. Not until the twentieth century, however, did it really begin to support and regulate whole sectors of American industry on a continuing, routine basis.

In his well-known textbook *Economics,* Nobel Prize-winning economist Paul A. Samuelson observes the following: "Each period of emergency, each war, each depression, expands the activity of government." In terms of controls and regulations, indirect and direct subsidies, and even out-

---

[1]Paul Samuelson, *Economics* (NY: McGraw Hill, 1980), p. 37.

right government ownership of corporations, every such period in American history has brought an increase in federal involvement in the private sector.

World War I
The government's interest in preserving national security—probably its most essential function—compels it to make a heavy investment in the defense industry. During times of war, the president has special authority to exert control over private enterprise. The first major expansion of federal activity during the twentieth century was brought on by World War I. The government took major initiatives in two areas: it gave financial aid to war industries and took control of some private enterprises. In both cases, the effects were felt long after the fighting was over.

Among the government "corporations" formed during World War I was the War Finance Corporation. It was created by Congress for the purpose of extending credit to essential war-related industries. During its six months of wartime operation, the War Finance Corporation advanced $71.4 million to private manufacturers. After the war ended in 1918, the corporation's charter was renewed, and its activities were expanded to the area of financial support for exports, primarily farm products. The War Finance Corporation was in fact not dissolved until 1929, by which time it had lent some $700 million. Even more importantly, it provided a model for future support agencies.

Also during World War I, the government for the first time took over a large private industry and operated it on its own. To speed the transportation of goods and materials, President Woodrow Wilson invoked his wartime powers to take control of the nation's railroads. For more than two years, January 1918–February 1920, Washington ran the entire U.S. train system. (The average cost of operation was estimated to be 83 percent higher under federal management than before the takeover.) Twice within fifteen years after the war, in 1919 and 1934, Congress considered whether to nationalize, or permanently take over the railroads. Although the proposal was rejected both times, the railroad has remained one of the most heavily subsidized industries in the United States. Beyond that, Wilson's takeover of the trains during World War I helped fuel an explosion of government activity in the private sector.

The Depression and New Deal

The stock market crash of 1929 created a national emergency at least as grave as that of World War I. Professor Samuelson's observation that periods of emergency have led to the expansion of U.S. federal authority is perhaps most evident in the case of the Great Depression of the 1930s. To pull the nation out of its economic crisis, President Franklin Roosevelt, with the help of scores of advisers, instituted a series of recovery measures referred to collectively as the New Deal. Roosevelt's New Deal policies marked a major turning point in American history. The federal government assumed an unprecedented amount of responsibility for the social and economic well-being of the public. The various programs of the New Deal represented the government's deepest and widest penetration into the private sector.

This penetration required a basic change in the government's policy-making structure. Scores of federal agencies and public corporations were formed to provide assistance to essential industries and the general citizenry. Many of them continued to operate for decades after the depression. The U.S. economic system would never be the same.

At the heart of early New Deal policy—aimed at relief and recovery rather than long-term reform—were the National Industrial Recovery Act and the Agricultural Adjustment Act, both passed by Congress in 1933. These

[31]

In the 1930s the TVA helped to build
many dams such as this one on the
Clinch River near Knoxville, Tennessee.

bills called for the creation of agencies to help manufacturers and farmers. The Agricultural Adjustment Agency (AAA) was designed to raise farm prices and pay growers to cut production or reduce their acreage. Although the AAA had only a limited effect on the nation's overall recovery, it was a great boost to farmers. The National Recovery Administration (NRA) sought to create a better climate for business and industry, but the controversial agency was declared unconstitutional by the Supreme Court in 1935. The Public Works Administration (PWA) was also created by the industrial recovery act, and it had a longer life. Before its dissolution in the 1940s, the PWA had spent more than $4 billion on long-term construction projects.

Another important New Deal agency was the Reconstruction Finance Corporation (RFC). It was actually formed in 1932 by President Herbert Hoover, and it was modeled on Wilson's War Finance Corporation. The RFC was created "to aid in financing agriculture, commerce . . . industry . . . and small business." Through the New Deal and until it was disbanded in 1957, the agency lent billions of dollars for those purposes.

The second phase of New Deal policy—aimed at creating reforms to keep the economy healthy in the long term—was highlighted by the establishment of the Tennessee Valley Authority (TVA). The TVA is a large-scale program for the development of an entire region through its water resources. The Works Progress Administration (WPA) was another reform initiative. Its purpose was to create worthwhile jobs for the unemployed. The WPA was terminated during World War II; the TVA still exists today.

Because of all the assistance programs begun in the New Deal, the total amount of domestic economic aid provided by the U.S. government increased from $232 million in 1932 (before Roosevelt took office) to more than $1 billion in 1934.

[33]

Also affecting private industry were powerful new institutions that greatly expanded the government's control. Agencies were established to regulate commerce and trade, labor relations, stocks and bonds, and almost every other area of business.

All in all, the New Deal did so much to increase the government's social responsibility and economic authority that even some members of Roosevelt's own administration warned that his programs would create a communistic state.

World War II

World War II—the third major emergency faced by the United States in the twentieth century—saw even further advancement of government control over the economy. Federal commissions and agencies were set up to coordinate and supervise the production of war materials as well as basic industrial goods. The government's first task was to induce industry to expand and convert its peacetime facilities into plants for the manufacture of arms. Then it had to channel the war matériel, as well as labor, into the overall war effort. Last, but not least, the government had to make sure that basic economic needs were met at home. This required careful allocation (distribution) of commodities and, eventually, a rationing system of fixed monthly or weekly allowances for food, gasoline, and other commodities.

One way the government exercised its wartime authority was to issue "blanket orders," such as one that forbade production of passenger cars. At the same time, it spent many billions of dollars in subsidies, supports, and complicated benefits to spur private industry. The Reconstruction Finance Corporation, which was still in existence, helped fulfill the needs of the defense economy. There were tax incentives and a variety of other programs to help private manufacturers. Federal spending jumped significantly during the war years.

One industry that especially benefited from the American effort in World War II was shipbuilding. Beginning in 1936, the U.S. Maritime Commission subsidized the construction and operation of ships for certain types of foreign trade. Although this resulted in a small number of new and efficient vessels, the real progress took place during the war years, 1939–1945. New plants, modern machinery, and innovative production systems—all with the help of the government—drastically cut the amount of time needed to build a ship. The number of new vessels increased rapidly.

In short, World War II had a far-reaching effect on American private enterprise. Many underdeveloped regions of the country benefited from the employment and business provided by new factories. In parts of the South and West especially, new plants brought lasting industrialization and greater prosperity. And, like the New Deal, World War II forced American business and government to work even more closely together.

The economy was mixing fast.

Post-1945

Since the last major emergency of the twentieth century—World War II—the government has adopted a somewhat different approach to industrial and agricultural subsidies. Although a great many of today's subsidy programs were begun before the war, the forms in which the benefits are given and the purposes they serve have changed. The basic difference is that the government began to use subsidies more as a *tool*.

In the past, aid and incentives for private industry had been given primarily to meet an urgent need. In the 1800s, they were used to help American industries through their infancy. In the first half of the twentieth century, they were used to help the nation through the emergencies of World War I, the Great Depression, and World War II. During the post-1945 period, however, the government began to realize how it might use subsidies to serve more basic, day-to-day purposes. Most importantly, they could be used to enhance the quality of life, to ensure the production of essential goods and services, and to promote the public good. At the same time, the government would be exerting more control over the economy as a whole. It could speed up production in one area and slow it down in another. It could protect people in business, and it could spur economic growth.

Thus, subsidies began to serve a wider variety of public objectives. Hundreds of programs were established to more closely and routinely regulate the economy—individual industries, geographical areas, and whole segments of the population. Federal subsidies to local governments, private industries, small firms, and even individuals became more complex and more commonplace. The government assumed greater control, and the private sector became more dependent.

In the late 1940s and 1950s, the arms industry was again a major recipient of government aid. As a result of the Cold War with the Soviet Union, huge companies were created to build up the nation's defensive armaments. At that time also, the U.S. space program was spawned to compete with that of the Soviet Union. Both the weapons producers and the fledgling aerospace industry depended on contracts from the federal government. The regions in which they were centered could not survive economically without the government's business.

The postwar expansion of federal authority also touched the social well-being of the American people. In 1946, Congress passed the Full Employment Act, which declared that it was the "responsibility of the Federal Government to use all practical means . . . to promote maximum employment, production, and purchasing power." Although whole new areas of federally-sponsored assistance were born during the 1950s, President Dwight Eisenhower frequently expressed his displeasure at what he regarded as a trend toward socialism.

The next major period of growth in federal aid came during the presidencies of John Kennedy and Lyndon Johnson in the 1960s. In the tradition of Roosevelt's New Deal, Kennedy's New Frontier and Johnson's Great Society programs called for a broad range of new domestic subsidy programs. The number and cost of grants grew faster between 1960 and 1968 than in any other period since the New Deal. Federal spending tripled. Although the emphasis was again on social benefits, private industry also got a shot in the arm. The goal of providing public housing, for example, meant more federal contracts for construction companies. Trade, transportation, aerospace, and other important industries benefited significantly from legislation passed during the Kennedy-Johnson era.

The 1970s—Bailouts

Even though the U.S. economy had been mixing rapidly for several decades, and even though federal subsidy programs had become a multi-billion-dollar expense, the 1970s brought another twist—and another step ahead—in the growth of the subsidized economy. Private industry had become so dependent on help from Washington that now individual companies were coming to the government for emergency aid.

In 1970, the Penn Central Railroad was running out of money and asked the federal government to guarantee $200 million in loans. The request could be granted, said Penn, under terms of a law passed during the Korean War;

that legislation allowed private companies to borrow from the federal treasury for defense purposes. A lengthy debate ensued, but Congress and the administration of President Richard Nixon turned the company down. In mid-June, Penn Central declared bankruptcy. Then the government stepped in and offered to guarantee repayment of loans up to $125 million.

The next year, another company came to Washington with its hand out. The Lockheed Aircraft Corporation was not in as much trouble as Penn Central, but it had lost $500 million in fulfilling four government contracts for military aircraft. Then, in trying to produce its Tri-Star L-1011 commercial jumbo jet, Lockheed was again running into financial trouble. Perhaps fearful for the entire U.S. airline industry, the Nixon administration this time came out in favor of assistance. Congress narrowly passed a bill providing Lockheed with $250 million in loan guarantees. By late 1977, the company had recovered financially and repaid all of its debts under the government guarantee.

The third major U.S. company to ask for emergency federal aid in the 1970s was, of course, Chrysler. The subsidized economy had come a long way since the time when 15 miles per hour was considered "breakneck speed." The mixture of free enterprise and government control had grown thick indeed.

CHAPTER 5

Subsidies – the Major Forms

As the role of the federal government expanded further and further, and as the economy became more "mixed," the flow of government subsidies to private industry grew faster and heavier. Support and promotion programs popped up everywhere, touching all sizes and types of industries and businesses. They came in an endless variety of new forms— often ingenious, often ill-conceived.

To make sense of the literally hundreds of U.S. federal subsidy programs now in existence, it is useful to group them in five major categories: cash payments; loans and credit; tax benefits; free or inexpensive services; and other devices. Each type works differently, each serves a different purpose, and each has different advantages and disadvantages. Although a particular kind of business might benefit from subsidies in all five categories, some industries receive the majority of their assistance from just one.

Cash Payments

The simplest and most direct form of subsidy provided by the federal government is a cash payment. Because it involves a fixed sum of money, this type of assistance has several advantages. The government knows exactly how much it is paying out and can maintain tighter control over its expenditures. Conditions and requirements are easily enforced, because the payments can be simply shut off if the recipient does not comply.

American agriculture receives a considerable amount of direct federal money each year. Farmers are paid to produce such essential crops as sugar, cotton, wheat, and wool. They may also receive funds for limiting their output, reducing their acreage, and using soil conservation techniques. Other industries that receive heavy cash payments are shipbuilding, aircraft construction, and exporting.

Compared with the other types of subsidies, however, the total federal expenditure on direct cash payments is very small. They are made only for a few business activities. The main reason for this is that any government agency making a direct cash subsidy must justify it to Congress, where public opinion comes to bear. An agency will not propose such an aid program unless it has reached a strong conclusion that the industry truly serves a vital public interest. Moreover, cash payments are the only form of subsidy specifically identified in the U.S. federal budget. Every appropriation is closely scrutinized by the Senate and House of Representatives. Many companies and industries, therefore, prefer more indirect forms of assistance. There is less public and congressional attention; the conditions and requirements are more difficult to enforce; and the subsidies are harder to shut off.

Loans and Credit Guarantees
The government also helps industry and agriculture by making direct loans to individual enterprises or by guaranteeing loans from banks and other private investors. In the

case of loan guarantees, the government promises repayment if the company cannot meet its obligation. Direct loans and credit guarantees induce businesses to undertake activities that are good for the public but are very risky financially. Because they are risky, it would be hard to find a private lender. When the government gives a direct loan it charges a lower interest rate than a bank or other private lender. When it provides a loan guarantee—as in the case of Chrysler—it allows the recipient to borrow money that no one would otherwise lend.

Housing construction, especially in the inner city where banks are reluctant to give credit, receives a large part of the government's loans and loan guarantees. Economic development in rural areas, exporting companies, and some small businesses also receive substantial credit benefits.

In 1981, the total amount of federal credit by direct and guaranteed loans advanced to nearly $80 billion. The year before it was only about $56 billion. Altogether, by the end of 1981, some $500 billion was still outstanding in unpaid debts.

Tax Benefits
To induce businesses to invest in certain types of activities, the government also gives a wide variety of tax breaks—deductions, reductions, exemptions, credits, and other special mechanisms—to lighten the burden. The U.S. tax code is thick with provisions benefiting many different business activities. Companies can more easily afford to make new investments, meet maintenance costs, and aggressively develop the business.

The industries that benefit most from U.S. federal tax help are oil and mining. Oil exploration and production are promoted by a complicated benefit called the oil depletion allowance. This is based on the declining value of an oil field as more oil is pumped out. Timber and other natural resources, agriculture, transportation, international trade, commerce, and economic development also get major tax help from Washington.

Tax benefits can be a powerful inducement for a particular industry, but they are probably the most difficult form of subsidy for the government to control. Because they do not *look* like subsidies, business executives like them. Because they do not appear costly, the government likes them. For the same reasons, however, it is hard to know how effective they are, and it is difficult to calculate their overall cost to the government. Finally, when they get out of hand—and many insist they have—individuals and companies that do not get the same benefits complain about "loopholes" that allow companies to escape some of their tax obligations.

Services

Perhaps the least recognized and least appreciated way in which the federal government helps private industry—but still a major form of subsidy—is the provision of essential services for free or at a greatly reduced cost. The prime example is mail service. The U.S. Postal Service is heavily financed by the federal treasury. The expense of delivering a letter or package is not nearly covered by the amount the sender pays in postage. Thus, publishers of newspapers and magazines, as well as companies that advertise through the mail, get a big financial boost from the government.

The postal system is not the only government service that benefits private industry. Water and waste disposal systems, air traffic control, harbor maintenance, management advice and technical assistance, and the publication of statistical reports and economic data are just some of the other useful services the government provides for free or at a relatively low cost. It has even been argued that a free educational system is a subsidy for private industry, because many employees—from blue collar workers to upper management—receive important training (such as reading and writing) in public schools. Although public schools are financed primarily by local government, Washington does help out. In fact, the federal government also gives financial assistance to private schools.

From these examples, one important fact emerges. The cost of service-subsidies and their effectiveness in promoting essential business activities are very difficult, probably impossible, to measure.

Other Benefits

Finally, the government provides indirect subsidies in a great many ways that do not fall into the other major categories. These, too, are difficult to evaluate in terms of cost and effectiveness. For example, the government develops new markets for U.S. foreign trade in the course of diplomatic negotiations. It establishes import tariffs, or taxes on foreign-produced goods brought into America. And it sells its own surplus goods at low prices.

Perhaps most importantly, the government awards contracts. It assumes the role of customer, paying a company to make something it needs, often military equipment. When a private firm wins a federal contract to build fighter planes or a nuclear-powered submarine, for example, it reaps valuable benefits. Many companies actually survive on the work they do for the government. They do not always earn a big profit, but the basic research and development are often valuable for future projects. Moreover, the awarding of the contract is a big plus for the community. Residents are employed, people move in, businesses grow, and the local government takes in additional money. More services—such as sewers, roads, public transportation, and new schools—can then be afforded. In short, a government contract is a kind of indirect subsidy for the area in which the company is located.

These, then, are the basic ways in which the U.S. federal government subsidizes private industry. The following chapter takes a closer look at who gets the subsidies and how they work.

CHAPTER 6

Guns, Butter, and Wheels

The three sectors of the American economy that depend most heavily on federal spending are defense, agriculture, and transportation. From the earliest days of the republic, the government has recognized that all three are essential to the well-being of the people. The defense industry manufactures the weapons and other equipment necessary for national security. Agriculture produces the fruits, vegetables, grains, and dairy products that feed the people. And transportation is essential for commerce, commuting to work, and basic communication among all regions of the land. Because guns, butter, and wheels are so vital to the public, the government has supported them more generously and more openly than other areas of the economy.

Although all three of these sectors survive on the good graces of the government, they are in somewhat different situations. Arms manufacturers get most of their money as payment under federal contract, while agriculture and transportation rely on a variety of assistance and support programs. The defense industry also stands out as the one

[45]

*President Reagan's determination to maintain
a high level of defense spending is
depicted here, with the suggestion that
the domestic budget, or "butter," be
downgraded to the status of "oleo margarine."*

area that President Reagan was most reluctant to cut in his budgets.

Defense
Maintaining a strong national defense has always been a primary objective of the government. Every year when the president and his advisers plan the federal budget and submit it to Congress for approval, a large portion is set aside for military spending. Other than direct benefit payments to individuals (social security, unemployment insurance, disability insurance, and other social programs), defense spending makes up the biggest slice of the budget pie. In fiscal 1980, just under 25¢ of every dollar spent by the government went to national defense; that came to about $143 billion. In 1981, the figure reached more than $170 billion. And for 1982, Congress agreed to an appropriation of about $200 billion—well over 27¢ of every federal dollar.

Money laid aside for national defense is spent in several different areas. Most of the money comes under the control of the Department of Defense, which divides it up according to need. A large portion goes to paying military personnel, operating military facilities (such as army, navy, and air force bases), and maintaining military equipment. An even heftier amount, however, goes to build new weapons, such as planes, ships, submarines, missiles, and sophisticated defense systems. Private firms are hired to do research, development, and testing. The government, of course, then spends enormous sums to buy the equipment. Companies such as General Dynamics Corporation, McDonnell Douglas, United Technologies, and General Electric get federal contracts totaling several billion dollars every year.

In addition to lucrative contracts, Washington showers other benefits on the defense industry. Arms manufacturers are provided direct loans and loan guarantees. They often use government-owned plants and equipment at no charge. They can claim tax deductions for money invested in basic research and development. Sometimes the government even pays for research not under contract. With all these subsidies, arms manufacturers often can earn profits without taking major financial risks.

Agriculture

Like a strong national defense, efficient and productive agriculture is a top U.S. priority. The health of the nation literally depends on the quality and quantity of the natural produce it consumes. Annual yields of fruits, vegetables, grains, and dairy goods have a major effect on the nation's overall economy. The United States is one of the world's largest producers of farm products, and foreign sales bring in important revenue. Millions of people all over the world depend on food grown in America.

For these reasons, the agricultural sector receives massive federal support. Agricultural subsidies serve a great many purposes: to make sure enough commodities are produced for domestic and foreign markets; to improve health, nutrition, and food safety; to make sure farmers are paid fairly for their goods; and to keep prices stable.

Subsidies to American farmers are as old as the nation itself. In the years after independence, the U.S. government began giving land to farmers or selling it to them at cheap prices. In subsequent decades, it founded agricultural colleges and institutions. It created agencies to lend farmers money. And it brought electricity to many farms. Still, it was not until Franklin Roosevelt's New Deal that the government began to help in a *really* big way. Whole new support programs were devised and put into operation. Most of the agricultural subsidies in existence today had their origin during the 1930s. They remain both plentiful and costly. Before looking at them in closer detail, it would be useful to consider some of the unique characteristics of the American farming business.

There are an estimated 2 million commercial farms (farms that sell their produce) in the United States today. They produce wheat, corn, and other grains in the Midwest; cotton, tobacco, and peanuts in the South; dairy products in the Northeast and Great Lake states; citrus fruits in California and Florida; and many, many other commodities across the land. Despite this great diversity, however, there are still a vast number of farmers producing each agricultural commodity. The competition is very keen.

Another problem for the commercial farmer is that fruits, vegetables, and dairy products do not last very long. They spoil. This, along with intense competition, leaves the farmer in a position unlike that of any other person in business. The farmer has very little control over how much he will be paid for his goods. In other industries, the manufacturer can force prices higher by offering fewer goods for sale—in other words, by withholding them from the market. Because the goods become scarcer, they are more valuable to potential buyers, who are then willing to pay higher prices. A commercial farmer cannot do this for two reasons: first, his many competitors might be willing to sell the same goods for less money; second, many farm products cannot be withheld from the market simply because they will spoil.

Recognizing the unique situation of the American farmer, the federal government during the 1930s began creating a whole new series of assistance programs, most of which are still in operation. The major agricultural subsidies today are for the purpose of "farm income stabilization." That is, they help stabilize the income of farmers. This is accomplished in two ways: 1) by saving the farmer from economic collapse due to a bad crop, flooding, drought, the high cost of machinery and supplies, the inability to sell, or any other reason; and 2) keeping income distributed fairly between big farms and small farms, and among farmers in the various regions of the country. Farm income stabilization subsidies include crop insurance against loss from natural disaster, special loans in case of an emergency, and, most importantly, *price supports.*

A price support is a guaranteed minimum price established by the federal government for a particular commodity. The farmer can be sure that he will receive a certain amount of money for, say, every bushel of corn he produces. No matter how little a farmer would receive on the free market, he or she can rely on getting the minimum price guaranteed by the government. How does the government decide what the minimum price should be? It is a complicated—and arbitrary—calculation. Basically, the government looks at the cost to the farmer of buying other industrial products over a certain period of years. Then it looks at the prices the farmer received for his bushel of corn over the same time period. It will then set the guaranteed minimum price so that the sale of one bushel will bring enough money to buy the same amount of other products as in the past.

This is already a big help to farmers, but how is it a subsidy? What actual financial *aid* does the government provide?

Consider the following situation: What if the government declares that the minimum price for a bushel of corn is five dollars, but the average selling price would otherwise be only three dollars? People stop buying corn, and the excess ends up just lying around in silos. There is, in other words, a large surplus.

[50]

This creates a problem. What if *you* are the farmer with the thousands—or even millions—of unsold bushels of corn? You have no income at all. Here is where the government steps in to help. It prevents such an occurrence in two ways: 1) it buys up the surplus goods at the established minimum price; or 2) it requires farmers to cut production enough to eliminate any possible surplus in the future (it actually pays some farmers *not* to produce).

The situation described above, is, in fact, a very common one. In 1981, the U.S. government paid out more than $3 billion in its farm support programs. About half the total agricultural output of the United States is protected by price supports. Some commodities—including cotton, wheat, corn, dairy products, and others—are guaranteed price protection by law. Certain others may be protected if the Secretary of Agriculture deems it necessary.

In addition to price supports and other farm income stabilization programs, the federal government subsidizes agriculture in several ways. It carries out research programs to increase crop yields. It runs programs to prevent the development and spread of diseases and pests that might damage crops. And it gives tax breaks for certain expenses and profits. All told, the government spends billions of dollars every year on formal agricultural subsidies. Beyond that, some farmers get help from other subsidy programs, such as aid for small businesses.

In their efforts to cut government spending, President Reagan and budget adviser David Stockman did not spare the agricultural community. Beginning with the budget for fiscal 1982, hundreds of millions of dollars were cut from farm subsidies. One of the first and largest cuts announced by the new Reagan administration was in dairy price supports. Reagan's experts felt that the price supports had encouraged dairy farmers to overproduce and had forced the government to buy up huge surpluses, at the expense of

the taxpayer. By cancelling an increase in dairy price supports scheduled for April 1, 1981, Reagan saved hundreds of millions of dollars.

Another agricultural subsidy program cut by Reagan was the Farmers Home Administration (FHA). The FHA makes special loans, particularly to farmers in small rural communities, to plant crops or recover from an adverse weather season. The FHA also helps build water and sewage systems in small towns. Out of its $14.5 billion budget for the previous year, Reagan cut about $100 million for 1982.

Transportation
A reliable system of transportation fulfills two basic needs of any nation: it meets the personal needs of the people, and it helps the economy run smoothly. Because the United States covers so large an area, the development of an adequate transportation network has long been a major problem and a basic goal. In many other countries, rail and air service are run by the government. In the United States, the construction and operation of the various forms of transportation have, for the most part, been left to private enterprise. At the same time, the U.S. government has assisted the transportation industry by granting large subsidies.

A bumper harvest of corn in Iowa
was piled on the ground when
the local grain elevator was full.
Agricultural subsidies help
control the price of commodities
in circumstances such as this.

[53]

In fact, transportation on the ground, in the air, and on the sea together receive more money in federal subsidies than any other U.S. industrial sector. The purpose of that aid is three-fold: 1) to develop and maintain the systems needed for commerce and public convenience; 2) to help ensure that they are safe, reliable, and efficient; and 3) to keep transportation programs and policies consistent with the nation's economic, social, and environmental goals. Not counting loans and tax credits, the federal government spent nearly $25 billion on budgeted transportation programs in 1981.

Land. Trucking and other kinds of commercial vehicle transportation benefit greatly from the government's expenditures on the highway system. In 1981, the federal government spent more than $7.5 billion on the construction, improvement, and maintenance of highways. (Most roads, however, are paid for by local and state governments.) Although commercial vehicles do pay taxes, the amount does not approach the cost to Washington of building and maintaining federal highways. In addition, the government runs programs to improve highway safety, a benefit to individuals and businesses alike.

The second largest contribution of the government to ground transportation is for railroads. Since the Civil War, the nation's many small railroad lines have been gradually consolidated into large transcontinental systems. These interstate networks receive tremendous subsidies from the government. The National Railroad Passenger Corporation (Amtrak) relies on nearly $1 billion in subsidies from Washington per year; passenger fares cover only about 50 percent of the railroad's operating costs.

Urban mass transit is another important part of the land transportation network. Subways, buses, trolleys, and other systems carry millions of people to work every day, and local funding does not nearly cover the cost. Washington contributes about $4 billion a year to the construction, modernization, safety, and energy efficiency of such systems.

Air. Ever since the beginning of air transportation, the U.S. government has subsidized the design and construction of new planes. For example, it spent more than $1 billion for the development of a supersonic plane before the project was discontinued in 1972. Private companies also derive incidental benefits from government spending on defense and aerospace. Research in these areas has brought important innovations in commercial air transport. Beyond that, the government provides operating subsidies to some airlines, builds and maintains airport facilities, and runs the air navigation and air traffic control systems. Budgeted air transportation outlays by the government in 1981 came to about $4 billion.

Sea. Washington pays about $3 billion a year in maritime subsidies. Shipbuilders and ship operators receive cash directly. Loans and loan guarantees are also awarded. In addition, the government maintains inland waterways, harbors, and dock facilities. Finally, it helps the shipping industry by establishing preferential regulations and policies for foreign and coastal trade.

The transportation budget was one of the areas most seriously slashed by Ronald Reagan for 1982. Federal highway construction was cut by $244 million, with a total proposed reduction of $12.6 billion between 1982 and 1986. Conrail, the railroad system that provides freight and passenger service in the Northeast—and which had survived on government money—would lose *all* its federal support after 1982. Amtrak passengers would have to pay a greater percentage—up to 80 percent—of the railroad's operating costs. Mass transit grants in general would be cut by $360 million in 1982, a total of $4.6 billion from 1981 through 1986, and eventually would be wiped out completely if Reagan has his way. Funds for the construction and expansion of airports would be reduced by one-third between 1981 and 1986. The list goes on and on.

Despite the controversies stirred by these and other budget cuts, President Reagan's economic proposals emphasized some questions that had been in the minds of the public for several years. Was government trying to do too much? Was it assuming too much responsibility for social services? In terms of business and industry, was it providing too many protections? Was it pampering the private sector, restricting it, or both?

How effective are government subsidies, anyway? Do they bring the desired results in a particular industry? For society as a whole? Do they cost too much? What are their advantages and disadvantages? What are the alternatives?

The following chapter looks at both sides of these issues—the pros and the cons.

CHAPTER 7

The Two Sides of the Coin

Coretta Scott King, the widow of slain civil rights leader Martin Luther King, Jr., commented in the spring of 1968 on the economic and social policies of the U.S. government. Mrs. King said, "Our Congress passes laws which subsidize corporations, farms, oil companies, airlines, and houses for suburbia, but when it turns its attention to the poor, it suddenly becomes concerned about balancing the budget."

Over the years, the use of federal subsidies has come under heavy attack. The most common criticism, like that of Mrs. King's, is that they are inequitable, that they unfairly favor one group at the expense of another. By their very nature, subsidies give advantage to particular interests in society. Whether to moneyed business interests over the poor, or to large conglomerates over smaller competitors, the advantage has no doubt been unfair in many instances.

At the same time, however, the growth of the subsidized economy coincided with a very definite trend toward greater government assistance for the poor and disadvantaged. Many of the subsidy programs born during the

1930s were designed specifically to get people working—
for fair wages and in humane conditions. In the decades
since, the government has taken on more and more responsibility for the social and economic needs of the people.
Subsidies have served a wider and wider range of public
objectives.

The debate over government subsidies is a many-sided
one. It is not simply a matter of being for subsidies or
against subsidies. There are a variety of different answers
to a host of different questions. And, as shown in the following pages, there are at least two sides to every issue.
Quite certainly, government subsidies serve useful purposes
and have some favorable results. Just as certainly, they
have major drawbacks and some inherent disadvantages.
The problem is to sort out the jumble and judge for one-
self.

To help sort out the jumble, one can look at three general areas of debate. While all three are closely related,
they each focus on the issue from a different angle, and
they each bring different questions to bear.

First, are the *right* objectives being pursued? Are they
fair? Mrs. King, for example, claims they are not. She and
other social critics have maintained that the needs of at
least some of the people are being misunderstood, distorted,
or simply ignored. Similarly, some businesses and industries maintain that they are not getting enough federal help
while others are getting more than they need.

The conflict between the interests
of the farmer, who receives
subsidies for not growing crops,
and the interests of the poor
is illustrated in this cartoon.

[59]

Second, are the subsidy programs in operation today *effective* in meeting those objectives? For example, do price supports really help farmers? All farmers? In short, do subsidy programs accomplish what they are intended for?

And finally, what are the overall consequences of a subsidized economy? Has the government grown too big and powerful? Or should it assume even greater responsibility? Should it leave business and industry entirely to private concerns? Or should it help out and keep closer tabs on the economic balance?

Objectives

The growth of the subsidized economy could not have occurred without some strong reasons for the ever-increasing outlay of federal money. Government subsidies are intended to serve several important purposes, all of which appear to be constructive and desirable—at least on the surface. Many of them have already been discussed, but it is useful to list and review these overall objectives.

- To help private enterprise produce things it ordinarily would not produce in a purely capitalistic, profit-motivated system. Some projects are so huge or so novel that no private company would undertake them without financial help. Likewise, some things are so expensive to produce and the chances of making money so small that no private company would invest in the business without backing. Examples of this are the space program, highways and transportation systems, and new energy technology. Because the government thinks these things are important, it subsidizes companies to work in these areas.
- To help make sure that essential goods and services are produced in sufficient amounts to meet the needs of the people. Agricultural subsidies are a good example—they are intended to keep enough fruits, vegetables, breads, and dairy products on supermarket shelves.

- To promote development and growth, of both existing industries and new ones. The government provides a great deal of subsidy help, in various forms, for research, testing, and overall expansion into new areas and innovative production methods.
- To protect businesses from financial or natural disaster. Washington has used subsidies to help companies like Chrysler avoid bankruptcy, and it routinely insures farmers against drought, storms, and other acts of God.
- To help maintain competitive balance. Subsidies are one device used by the federal government to keep companies on a relatively equal footing so that the big firms will not put the little ones out of business. The Small Business Administration lends millions of dollars every year to help entrepreneurs start private businesses. Special tax regulations, price supports, and other programs are designed to preserve a spirit of healthy competition.

In terms of our "mixed" economy, then, government subsidies are intended to keep things glued together. As an economic device, they indeed form a strong bond between the public and private sectors. Individually, the objectives listed above are hard to fault. Cooperation between the government and the private sector seems like a good way to accomplish them.

Taken as a group, however, the objectives listed above raise some serious doubts. Are they too ambitious? Is it possible to achieve all of them? Can the government possibly manage all the programs necessary to do so? More importantly, what is *sacrificed* in order to achieve them? Who pays the price?

In October 1979, President Jimmy Carter appointed forty-five private citizens to consider the important issues facing American society and to make recommendations for the next decade. Thirteen months later, the commission submitted its report, *A National Agenda for the Eighties*.

[61]

In the section on the economy, the commission addressed the question of vast federal subsidies to private business and industry, as well as to geographic regions and individual citizens. The report was critical of the government's general lack of direction and confusion of purpose. Said the commission,

> *There has been insufficient consideration given to the overall effect of these policies, and they have often worked at cross-purposes with one another or with broader policy goals. Systematic reviews of government activities are needed to prune or modify those that are unnecessary or inappropriate.*

The dangers of not recognizing the overall effects of federal subsidies—or any other kind of program—are many.

First of all, the government loses control of its own policies and resources. Congress and the executive branch admittedly have trouble enforcing federal requirements and monitoring the uses of federal subsidies. The great complexity of subsidy programs makes it almost impossible to ensure absolute efficiency. Companies take advantage. Abuses occur. The specific purposes of subsidy programs are not always met, and the overall objectives often come into conflict with each other. Indeed the overall objectives may be so broad and sweeping that they *have to* come into conflict. Perhaps it is impossible for a democratic government to design, operate, and control the programs necessary to accomplish all the objectives.

Another danger is that the private sector will become too dependent on government help. Some say this has already happened. They cite companies such as Chrysler, Penn Central, and Lockheed as examples of businesses that owe their very existence to the good graces of their rich Uncle Sam. But Uncle Sam is not rich enough to support the entire private sector, and a line has to be drawn some-

[62]

where. Moreover, industries in which too many companies rely on government help run the risk of losing their competitiveness. And if companies do not compete, fewer goods are produced and everyone suffers. (Or so the argument goes. The more general debate over free-market capitalism versus control by big government is discussed in a later section of this chapter.)

Finally, a subsidy system in disarray gives rise to unfairness. Companies and whole industries that do not need heavy support sometimes receive more subsidies than businesses that do need a lot of help. Even more troubling, however, is that important social goals may be sacrificed for the broad, overly ambitious, often conflicting economic objectives served by government subsidies. Mrs. King has maintained that the needs of the poor have been sacrificed to the wants of big business. Indeed it is easy to point out where money given to wealthy companies could have been used to provide services for the poor. For instance, oil companies have been granted "depletion allowances" while the poor in some cities had inadequate transportation for many years and were not able to seek jobs in outlying areas.

On the side of government, it can be argued that subsidies to private industry have important benefits for the poor—some directly and many indirectly. In 1964, Congress passed the Urban Mass Transportation Act, which provided vast sums of money to private companies for planning and constructing better transportation systems for cities. The companies certainly profited from these contracts, but the longer-lasting benefit was for the urban poor. More fundamentally, some say that subsidies to private industry, whether they *seem* fair or not, ultimately help everybody— including the poor—by keeping the nation's economy strong.

The final question, then, is this: Does *every* taxpayer get his or her money's worth from today's federal subsidy programs? The enormous funding Washington provides to

[63]

business and industry is largely paid for by taxes. Is the money being spent wisely?

Effectiveness

While subsidies in general are intended to meet the broad, overall objectives listed in the previous section, each program is also intended to serve narrower, specific purposes. The Small Business Administration is set up to help entrepreneurs begin businesses and keep them afloat. Agricultural price supports are designed to guarantee fair prices and maintain competition. Loans and loan guarantees for the housing industry are intended to make homes affordable, spur lumber and other related industries, and help rebuild decaying inner-city areas.

In weighing the pros and cons of a subsidized economy, a very basic question is whether the particular subsidy programs actually accomplish their specific aims. Even if the overall economic objectives were fair and practical, the question remains whether today's subsidy programs operate the way they are supposed to.

Again, there are no easy answers. Some subsidy programs are more efficient than others. Some are well-conceived and accomplish much of what they are intended to accomplish. Others are poorly designed, inefficiently managed, and doomed to failure. Moreover, it is difficult to judge the success of a subsidy program, because the concrete effects are not easy to measure. Expert economists devise complicated formulas and elaborate assessment techniques for studying the success or failure of various subsidy programs. They still disagree.

While it would take literally thousands of pages to assess all of the subsidy programs sponsored by the U.S. government, it might be interesting to look at one specific kind—farm price supports—in terms of its success or failure. How farm price supports work has already been explained in chapter 6. The many positive and fair-minded aspects of the program should be clear from that explanation, and farm price supports have in many ways been successful in accomplishing those goals. However, without using complex economic formulas, it is also easy to understand the many criticisms that have been leveled against them. It has been said that farm price supports do not get at the basic agricultural problems of the United States today, and for several reasons:

• By guaranteeing prices, the government controls production. When it pays farmers not to produce, quotas— or limits on production—are established. Although this does keep many farms in operation, they do not always run at full capacity. The land is not put to full use.

• By maintaining high prices and buying up surplus goods, the government encourages farmers to overproduce. Overproduction is itself one of the basic problems of American agriculture.

• The U.S. government buys huge amounts of surplus produce at staggering costs. In 1981, for example, it paid nearly *$1 billion* to buy more than 600 million pounds of surplus butter alone. In addition, it paid about $110 million (or $300,000 a day) to store the butter in refrigerated warehouses! Who pays the bill? Taxpayers.

• The guaranteed high prices are ultimately supported by consumers who pay more for the produce at the supermarket cash register. It is a heavy burden, which is not borne by the rich alone. Low-income families also have to buy food.

• Price supports have not substantially helped small, poor farmers. Because small farms produce little, a slightly higher price (albeit guaranteed) does not increase their income very much. Farmers that produce a great deal, on the other hand, increase their income substantially. Meanwhile, it is the large commercial farms that receive most of the benefits.

[65]

Some people would maintain that is important for the nation's general prosperity to support agriculture to the fullest. Agriculture is, after all, a very basic and vital sector of the economy. In response to that argument, one might point out that the 1920s and 1950s, two of the most prosperous decades in American history, were by no means boom periods for farmers. Even more telling is the argument that farm price supports—the most important federal subsidy program for American agriculture today—are not only ineffective, but also wasteful and unfair.

Whether farm price supports are a success or a failure, whether they should be abolished or preserved, remains open to question. There is, however, one important characteristic of price supports—and all other types of subsidies—that cannot be disputed. They do represent a radical departure from classical free-market, capitalist economics. By interfering in business and industry—either by guaranteeing high prices, providing loans and tax credits, or enforcing regulations—the government weakens the basic competitive framework of the free private enterprise system.

Free Enterprise versus Big Government

The United States government, it has been pointed out, is the biggest business in the world. It employs more people, handles more money, and produces more goods and services than any other single organization on earth. In fiscal 1980, total government spending—about $580 billion—amounted to more than 22 percent of all the goods and services provided by the nation. And the percentage has been increasing every year. However, in a competitive capitalist system, there is little need for heavy government participation. Indeed, according to the free market principles of Adam Smith, any interference is regarded as injurious.

That basic contradiction has fueled one of the most

[66]

fundamental, ongoing debates in American public life. On one hand, the United States has always leaned toward a pure capitalist approach. On the other hand, the government has gradually taken a greater and greater role in the economy. The growth of subsidies and government control have caused a "mixing" of the U.S. economy (see chapter 4). The recurring issue is whether or not the economy has become *too* mixed—whether we have strayed too far from the priciples of pure capitalism and free private enterprise.

In order to answer that question, it is first necessary to understand how that system is supposed to work and what it is supposed to accomplish. In theory, it has major points in its favor. Despite those theoretical advantages, however, free enterprise is fundamentally criticized on several counts. In looking at the pros and cons, the issue of government subsidies is ever-present. Throughout the explanation, one other point should be kept in mind: a pure system of free-market capitalism does not exist today, nor is it likely that it ever did exist. The choice to be made is somewhere *between* the extremes of pure free enterprise and dependence on big government.

The pure capitalist system is based on several governing principles: 1) all property and resources are owned by private citizens or organizations, not the government; 2) private businesses are free to choose their own areas of activity, buy necessary materials, produce the goods as they see fit, and sell them however they please; 3) the desire for profit is the motivation for production; and 4) there is free competition among rival businesses.

A basic feature of this system (in theory at least) is that it solves the basic economic problems and supplies all the needed goods of a society—without the government or anyone else mixing in. While the workings of it would be very complex in a country the size of the United States, it is basically very orderly. In a very simplified way, here is how it works:

Let's say three different companies are in the camera business. Each makes one kind of camera. Each camera takes pictures, of course, but each of them is also different. They have different features, such as special lenses, focusing devices, and speed controls, and they take pictures of varying quality. They also have different prices. The buying public, at the same time, has differing needs. Some people want better cameras and are willing to pay more money. Others are willing to settle for a cheaper model. All three cameras might be bought by one person or another, but the general public will buy only so many. The total number the public is willing to buy is called the "market" for cameras.

Now let's say that two of the camera models sell very well, but the third does not. In other words, the camera market only supports two of the companies. The third is losing money. It must either develop a new model that the public will buy in greater number (which might put another company in trouble), or else it must go into some other business, like slide projectors.

This is how, in a free-enterprise system, competition for the market is supposed to control production. Not just for cameras, but for everything—clothes, food, cars, machinery, etc. If the public needs something, a private company will be motivated to produce it by a desire to make more money. If the public does not want something— or if the price is too high—the company producing it will either go out of business, lower the price, or make something else. In this way, everything a society needs will be available in the right amount for the right price; there will be no waste.

It is, in theory, a very efficient and orderly system. The advantages (again, only in theory) are worth listing:

• It guarantees economic freedom. Private individuals and businesses are free to make their own decisions and choices. While mistakes can be costly because of the great competition, at least the decisions are made without interference by any authority. The spirit of freedom is the cornerstone of American democracy.

• It naturally produces and distributes everything the people need. Through the market system described above, the desire for profit leads private enterprise to produce all the goods and services a society desires (as if guided by Adam Smith's "invisible hand").

• The economy is dictated by the public. What goods are produced is ultimately determined by what the people want to buy. How much they cost is dictated by what the consumer is willing to pay. It is an economy "of the people, by the people, for the people."

Those who favor the principles of free-market capitalism argue that government subsidies interfere in the competitive process. Federal participation and control, they say, limit freedom and disrupt the natural production of needed goods. If, returning to the example of the cameras, the failing company were kept in business by government subsidies, its camera would continue to be produced. But the camera would be an unnecessary commodity, a waste of resources and labor. The public would be paying for that waste through taxes. If that were to occur in all industries, the waste and inefficiency would be a great load for the economy to carry. Moreover, if all three camera companies depended on government subsidies, they would lose their competitive spirit. Why compete? Why not produce a cheap product and charge high prices? Some say this is occurring throughout the U.S. private sector today.

Persuasive as these arguments seem, other views hold that a pure capitalist system cannot work in today's world. It is necessary, they maintain, for government to step in and keep the economy under control. Why? Some of the reasons might be clear from previous chapters:

• There are certain things that private companies could not, or would not produce even though they are for the good of society. As already noted, some projects are so expensive, so untried, or so financially risky that private companies would not undertake them without help.

• Competition ultimately breaks down. In seeking to gain an advantage over rival businesses, some companies would engage in dishonest or unfair activities—such as false advertising, bribery, etc. Or else all the companies might join together to cheat the public; they might all agree to produce shoddy goods and charge the same high price. In either case, the benefits of honest competition would be lost.

• Shifts from one area of production to another are not smooth. Looking again at the example of the cameras, the failing company could not immediately turn to some other industry. New equipment would have to be bought to manufacture a new product. Employees would have to be retrained. And new procedures would have to be put into operation. The transition might take months or years. Thus, moves into more profitable and needed industries are slowed. There are temporary imbalances and instability throughout the private sector.

• Modern technology means less competition. In many industries, new and expensive machinery keeps small firms out of business. Only large-scale operations survive. Automobiles are a good example. Whereas there used to be many different car manufacturers competing against each other, today in the United States there are only three major ones. The most important reason for this is the great cost of buying equipment and the enormous amount of labor needed to keep it running. This lack of competition means that only a few companies will monopolize whole markets. What happened to the economic freedom of the smaller companies?

To help overcome these problems, the government has tried to keep things going by providing subsidies and to control things by establishing rules and regulations. Whether the overall objectives of a subsidized economy are reasonable or not has already been considered. Whether subsidies accomplish their purposes or not has also been discussed. But even if the goals are sound and the programs effective, defenders of the capitalist system still argue that intervention by big government creates a serious danger.

The danger is that big government will become oppressive. That it will grow in size and power. That it will interfere in the everyday lives of ordinary people. Not only might it become unmanageable, inefficient, and costly, but—some say—it might begin to take away personal rights and privileges. That is still the most significant criticism of the Soviet, Chinese, and other Communist systems. In the United States, the court system and the spirit of the people stand against such an eventuality. Still, in 1980, candidate Ronald Reagan felt compelled to point out that government had gotten out of hand, that it was time to "get government off our backs."

These, in short, are the two sides of the subsidy issue. As shown, there are convincing arguments both for and against this practice. Certainly there are people who argue strongly for each position, and the debate goes on continuously. It can even be followed on a regular basis in newspapers and magazines. There are, as well, many other related issues in American public life from day to day. Two of the most important ones are discussed in chapter 8.

CHAPTER 8 | Regulations and Lobbying— Evil By-Products?

The growth of the subsidized economy has given rise to two activities which today have a profound effect on government, business, and the relationship between them. They both serve very useful functions, but like anything else, they are dangerous in excess. One is government regulation. The other is lobbying.

Government regulations are the thousands of laws, rules, controls, and procedures that the federal government imposes on private industry. Regulations in the automobile industry were at the center of the debate over the Chrysler bailout. There are also regulations for the design and production of planes, ships, factories, and houses. Federal regulations affect the food we eat, the water we drink, and even the air we breathe. Indeed there are very few things that we use or consume that are not produced under some degree of control by the government.

Lobbying is an effort by an organization or individual to influence the government on behalf of a particular industry, company, trade union, or other special interest group. Professional lobbyists—or members of the interest group

[72]

itself—try to persuade Congress or the White House to grant them special privileges, such as passing a favorable bill, providing a special subsidy, or repealing a burdensome regulation. Lobbying is an old practice, but in recent years it has become especially widespread. Today lobbying is carried out on behalf of every interest from dairy farming and trucking, to banking, consumerism, environmentalism, and gun control (both for and against).

The expansion of government regulation and lobbying are directly related to the growth of the subsidized economy. As the federal government bestowed greater and greater benefits on private industry, it also assumed greater control. Subsidies were often provided on the condition that certain practices would be followed. Regulations were drawn up and the industry had to comply. Even when it was not bestowing some special benefit, the government was creating regulatory agencies to meet the emergency needs of World War I, the Great Depression, and World War II. All in all, government subsidies and federal regulations grew up hand in hand.

Subsidies and regulations, in turn, gave birth to lobbying. As the government became more involved in the private sector, companies, industries, unions, and trade associations had more to gain or lose. Individually and together they began to lobby for their financial interests. Skilled lobbyists tried to exert pressure on public officials to get all kinds of subsidies—direct funding, tax breaks, and indirect benefits. They also sought to prevent passage of regulations that would be costly or difficult to follow. By 1979, the Clerk of the House of Representatives estimated that there were more than forty-seven hundred active registered lobbyists.

What useful purposes do regulations and lobbying serve for the general public? Have they gotten out of hand? How are they harmful? If they are, what is being done about them?

[73]

Regulations—A Closer Look

Government regulation has become a hot political issue. The general consensus among the public, government, and industry is that a reduction in the number and scope of federal regulations is sorely needed. Regulation has become something of a dirty word.

At the same time, it is important to keep in mind that government regulations can and do serve very useful functions. Even while the general outcry has been for a reduction in regulations, public opinion polls have consistently shown a desire for better government protection of human health and the environment. The American public has already been well served by federal regulations covering air and water pollution, food and drug safety, discrimination and minority rights, consumer protection, and other important social concerns. And the demand for stricter measures is still growing.

In addition to social goals, government regulations also serve basic and necessary economic functions. By issuing rules, establishing procedures, and creating standards for private industry to follow, the government helps control and coordinate the various sectors of the economy. It spurs production in areas that might otherwise be lacking. It prevents a single firm from monopolizing a particular industry. It establishes minimum wages and fair employment standards. In general, it helps guide the economy and make it grow.

For the dual purpose of promoting social benefits and maintaining economic efficiency, dozens of government agencies and departments have been created in the last forty years. Some are divisions of the cabinet within the executive branch and thereby under presidential authority. Others are independent and subject to controls by both the president and Congress. They have names like the Federal Trade Commission (FTC), Federal Communications Com-

[74]

mission (FCC), Food and Drug Administration (FDA), Environmental Protection Agency (EPA), and Occupational Safety and Health Administration (OSHA).

Despite all the useful purposes served by federal regulations, the feeling persists that they have become too numerous and often burdensome. Many are considered arbitrary, petty, unreasonable, and just plain unnecessary—not to mention expensive.

It is difficult to calculate exactly how much regulations cost the nation every year, but it is no doubt a staggering amount. In addition to all the money spent by the government to maintain regulatory agencies, study the need for new controls, and enforce the ones already in existence, vast sums are laid out by individual companies to comply with them. As in the case of the auto industry, meeting federal safety and pollution standards costs many millions of dollars in special production methods and machinery. In a televised address to the nation shortly after taking office, President Reagan estimated that "altogether, regulations . . . add $100 billion or more to the cost of the goods and services we buy."

Is it worth it? Do regulations benefit the average citizen enough to justify $100 billion? It is hard to think so. Companies have less capital to invest, their output declines in quantity and quality, and extra costs are passed on to the consumer. Also, foreign manufacturers gain an advantage: because their countries may not have as many regulations, they can produce their goods for less money and sell them at a lower price. This, of course, attracts buyers.

Once again, Chrysler is a useful case study. Although mismanagement was largely responsible for the company's near bankruptcy, the high cost of meeting government standards was also considered a major factor. If Chrysler had been forced to shut down, mass unemployment would have occurred, suppliers would have gone out of business, and

[75]

the nation's whole economy would have suffered (see chapter 1). It was a prospect that sent shudders through the industrial community.

For years, leaders of American business had been united in their call for a reduction in government controls. In 1980, they supported a candidate who agreed that federal regulations had put a stranglehold on American industry. As president, Ronald Reagan dedicated himself to limiting the role of government as regulator:

> *Government regulations impose an enormous burden on large and small business in America, discourage productivity, and contribute substantially to our current economic woes. It is my intention to curb the size and influence of the federal establishment.*

Reagan moved quickly to carry out his promise. He stopped the implementation of regulations passed in the final days of the Carter administration. He ordered government agencies to reassess and rejustify all existing and proposed regulations. And he appointed a special task force, headed by Vice President George Bush, to come up with workable strategies and concrete proposals for regulatory relief.

Lobbying—A Closer Look

The interests of lobby groups are not always selfish and financial. In petitioning for regulatory relief, for example, some businesses and industries are most concerned about the principle of freedom itself. While the lifting of federal controls saves a company money, mere freedom from federal authority is often a goal pursued for its own sake.

But aside from that, there are also lobby groups dedicated to social causes that will benefit everyone. In fact, they pursue many of the same goals as the government's own regulatory agencies—such as environmental protection, consumer rights, and so on. Groups such as Common Cause, the so-called citizens' lobby, Ralph Nader's various consumer organizations, the anti-abortion lobby, and the gun control lobby actually petition the government for *stricter* laws and regulations.

In further defense of lobbying, it must also be remembered that we all have the right—guaranteed by the Constitution—to free speech. Whether individually or together in a group, American citizens have the right to express their opinions clearly and forcefully on almost any issue they choose. Moreover, as a democratic society, we want to encourage a lively, ongoing debate on the controversial issues facing us. In this sense, the lobby movement can be a healthy one because the opinions of different groups are aired in abundance.

Despite all the potentially useful purposes served by lobbyists, the term today is applied more frequently to groups seeking special advantage than to groups promoting broader social reforms. Lobbyists are currently perceived as exerting too much pressure for their own narrow interests. As they grew bigger and better organized, they began to have political clout in Washington. Members of Congress could win or lose an election on the basis of a single issue; the support of one special interest group could carry that much weight. Elected representatives would grant special benefits, and taxpayers picked up the tab. Citizens genuinely concerned about the well-being of the nation—those who vote for what is best for everyone—began to lose *their* clout. The principle of government "for the people" was being lost to powerful, self-interested lobby groups.

The danger of excessive lobbying is well illustrated by the events surrounding the Federal Trade Commission (FTC) in 1979. The FTC is the government agency that protects the public from "deceptive and unfair" trade prac-

[77]

"MY ASSOCIATE AND I DID A LITTLE SELECTIVE SURGERY ON YOUR GUARD DOG."

*Complaints by lobbyists against the
Federal Trade Commission found
sympathetic ears in the Congress
with the result that the public's
"guard dog," the FTC, was in danger
of being made completely ineffective.*

tices by business and industry. Funds for the FTC are appropriated by Congress every year. In 1979, the FTC came under attack by several private interests, big and small. Oil companies joined together to try to stop an antitrust investigation by the agency. Leading automobile manufacturers attacked the FTC for a similar investigation in their industry. Funeral home directors banded together to stop the FTC from issuing certain regulations. So did used car dealers and advertising firms. In 1980, Congress considered closing down the FTC altogether. Twice during that year, for a total of three days, the agency had to cease operation for lack of money.

What happened? Why was the FTC almost shut down?

The business community maintained that the agency had been given too much authority and had become too aggressive. Maybe that was true. On the other hand, maybe the agency was really doing a good job in protecting the public from "deceptive and unfair" practices. In fact, maybe it was doing too good a job and members of Congress had just given in to pressure from the various interest groups to halt the agency's work. In that case, the good of the people would have been defeated by a group of selfish, overly powerful special interest groups.

This was not the first incident that aroused public concern over the growth of special interest lobbying. Several incidents during the administration of Richard Nixon made the public suspicious that its own best interests were being compromised. First it was disclosed that lobbyists for the International Telephone and Telegraph Company (ITT) had offered secret bribes to the government to stop an antitrust suit. Then, lobbyists for dairy farmers were reported to have donated $500,000 to President Nixon's 1972 reelection campaign fund after he had increased milk subsidies; this looked like another bribe payment.

[79]

The power of special interest lobbies was another aspect of the American system that candidate Ronald Reagan criticized during his campaign for the presidency. Like subsidies, regulations, and government itself, lobbying had gone too far, felt Reagan. The reason, as he proclaimed in his inaugural address, was that special interests had taken too much power from where it belongs—the people.

> *We hear so much of special interest groups. Well, our concern must be for a special interest group that has been too long neglected. It knows no sectional boundaries or ethnic and racial divisions, and it crosses political party lines. It is made up of men and women who raise our food, patrol our streets, man our mines and factories, teach our children, keep our homes, and heal us when we're sick—professionals, industrialists, shopkeepers, clerks, cabbies, and truckdrivers. They are, in short, "we the people."*

CHAPTER 9

Looking Back, Looking Ahead

Since the latter part of the nineteenth century, the U.S. economy has depended on a strong industrial base. Abundant natural resources, technological advancements, and efficient management have made American industry the most powerful in the world over the last century. At the same time, the American people have enjoyed a consistently higher standard of living than any other nation in the world. Even as the government was assuming a greater role in the affairs of private enterprise, American industry was the single most important reason for the nation's economic well-being, security from foreign aggression, and growing leadership in world affairs.

In the last decade, however, U.S. industry has had to face new and serious challenges. Natural resources once thought to be unlimited, such as oil, began to dwindle. Technological innovation seemed to slow in comparison with that of other rapidly-developing industrial giants, such as Japan. Organization and management, once looked up to and copied by foreign competitors, began to appear confused and outdated. The nation's productivity (defined as the average amount of material produced per man-hour of work) reached a peak around 1966 and has been declining ever since. As a result, the economic well-being of the American people has been jeopardized. Inflation, recession, high unemployment, high interest rates, and other symptoms of the general illness have made it harder for the average family to make ends meet. Finally, and not by coincidence, U.S. leadership in international affairs has slowly but surely been eroded.

The mixing of the economy and the growth of government subsidies have no doubt had a lot to do with both trends—the long-term strengthening and the more recent decline in U.S. prosperity and prestige. The subsidized economy has protected a great many businesses and helped countless others survive and continue producing; it has also helped larger corporations and whole industries try out new ideas, develop expensive technology, and engage in a wide range of activities they could not otherwise have afforded. On the other hand, government subsidies grew so numerous, so expensive, so complicated, and so difficult to control that they gradually got out of hand. Government itself began to realize that its own regulations were inhibiting production, that lobbies and special interest groups were exerting too much political pressure, and that the nation's economy was suffering.

Whatever the benefits and drawbacks of federal subsidies, one thing is clear: there is no turning back. The efforts of President Reagan to limit the role of government, cut certain subsidy programs, and bring back more free enterprise may or may not prove successful. But the system cannot be taken apart completely. Subsidies to private industry are too deeply woven into the pattern of the American economy. Even with all his cuts, President Reagan has been criticized for helping business too much. Subsidies are used to control and coordinate the entire industrial and agricultural sectors. In a mixed economy, government subsidies help glue things together.

For the future, then, the vital question is how to restore the industrial productivity and economic prosperity once enjoyed in the United States. What role should federal subsidies play? How can they be utilized fairly and efficiently?

Toward a Unified Industrial Policy
President Carter's Commission for a National Agenda, discussed in chapter 7, lodged a strong criticism of U.S. subsidy programs. "There has been insufficient consideration given to the overall effect of these policies," its report stated, "and they have often worked at cross purposes." In fact, the commission felt that such a lack of direction was symptomatic of the entire U.S. industrial sector. The special panel on the economy made the following observation:

> *The United States does not have* an *industrial policy comparable to the national industrial policies that exist in some other industrial nations. Rather, it has hundreds of policies that affect the various industries, each the result of decisions that usually arose in response to a particular problem or constituency.*

The point the panel was trying to make was that the U.S. economy is suffering from the absence of any unified, coherent program for industrial production. The government has taken an ever more active role in guiding the private sector, but its approach has been piecemeal. It has come to the aid of industries, workers, and even communities suffering from foreign competition. It has rushed in to rescue failing companies, such as Chrysler, Penn Central,

[83]

and Lockheed. But, for the most part, both the Congress and the presidents have either served special interests or merely *responded* to special circumstances. There has been a failure to devise any overall plan and then follow it through.

The first need, then, is simply better planning. Pressure has been building for a more farsighted policy, for a coherent plan of action, for a clearly marked path to follow. Some politicians have called for a Marshall Plan for American industry, a large-scale program to rebuild U.S. industry the way the economics of war-torn European countries were reconstructed after World War II. Their plea is not so much for a vast outlay of money as it is for a well-orchestrated, forward-looking approach to the revitalization of American industry. Such a policy need not interfere with the free-enterprise system, only make it more efficient.

Government, Business, and Labor

In the United States today, the performance of the economy is dictated by three major groups: government, business, and labor. Each one has a major influence on how well, or how poorly, private industry will do. Government exerts control by enforcing regulations and by granting or withholding subsidies; business management makes vital decisions regarding the operation and output of industries; and labor unions negotiate the terms and conditions under which employees will work.

The institutions of government, business, and labor have traditionally maintained what can be regarded as an adversarial relationship—a relationship where each one tends to pursue its own best interests. In doing so, they inevitably come into conflict. Management and labor constantly battle for power, with the government usually in the role of referee. And despite the government's enormous subsidies to private industry, its increasing involvement and authority give rise to conflicts, especially in the area of regulation. Finally, labor and government also find themselves at odds quite often. (The 1981 air traffic controllers strike was a good case in point. The 15,000-member Professional Air Traffic Controllers Organization staged the walkout in August 1981 in a dispute over a new contract. The controllers were government employees working for the Federal Aviation Administration, and the strike was therefore a violation of federal law. Government employees are not allowed to hold strikes. The confrontation lasted weeks, with the Reagan administration refusing to give in. The controllers were ultimately fired and replaced.)

This adversarial relationship is not entirely unhealthy. Compromises are hammered out, and no group becomes too powerful. However, the three-way tug-of-war has also been destructive. No group has been entirely to blame, but after all the years of confrontation, industrial production has begun to decline and the nation's economy has begun to falter. To reverse that trend, government, business, and labor must work more closely, in a spirit of cooperation. They each must think in terms of what is best for the entire nation and pursue those goals as partners.

The Benefits of Teamwork
Devising a national industrial policy is one area in which cooperation among government, business, and labor is vitally important. The benefits of coordinated planning have already been demonstrated in such countries as Japan, West Germany, Brazil, Mexico, and South Korea. In these nations, a close working relationship between government and business, with workers given a major voice in policy, has helped make rapid economic progress. They now compete with the United States in many industries.

Cooperative industrial planning has been especially successful in Japan and West Germany, both of which

[85]

rebuilt their economies after World War II and gradually became powerful industrialized nations. Their strategies were similar. The government singled out particular industries which it thought would be successful in world trade. It then invested great amounts of money for research and development in those areas, and exported heavily; imports for the designated products were restricted. Japan, for example, concentrated on steel and shipbuilding in the 1950s; automobile production in the 1960s; and computer technology since the mid-1970s. The Japanese government has special agencies for industry and trade, special financing, and overall planning. More importantly, business and labor work closely with the government. When Japanese officials make visits abroad or welcome foreign dignitaries at home, representatives of industry and labor are very often present.

As countries like Japan and West Germany began competing more successfully for world industrial markets, the United States began growing more envious of their development planning. The specific methods and goals that brought success to other countries may not be ideal for the United States. But, with increasing urgency, American business, labor, and government leaders have begun to realize that being partners rather than adversaries is essential for prosperity in the future. As certain commodities continue to grow scarce and as global economic conditions change, a joint effort will be the only way to adapt and compete successfully.

Subsidies—A Final Word
There have been a variety of proposals on how the new U.S. industrial policy should be formulated. The president's Commission for a National Agenda recommended that "a single Cabinet-level department" be created in the govern-

ment to develop and implement a comprehensive strategy. Congressman Henry Reuss of Wisconsin suggested that "independent teams from government, business, and labor be constituted to look into the problems of each of our major sectors" and then develop plans to remedy each problem. Senator Edward Kennedy of Massachusetts, when he was campaigning for the Democratic presidential nomination in 1980, proposed a new Reconstruction Finance Corporation (RFC)—like the one that operated during the Great Depression and World War II.

The issue, again, is subsidies—for whom, how much, and why. Should "winning" industries be picked out for intensive development, as in Japan, or should we first help the shaky ones get back on their feet? What form should the assistance take? How much control should the government have in the decision-making process?

The questions keep coming, and the answers remain elusive. But whatever it takes to revitalize U.S. industry, whatever it takes to restore productivity, and whatever it takes to keep America competitive with other nations, we do know that government subsidies will play a crucial role. The subsidized economy has grown too vast to be taken apart and rebuilt. The policies of presidents may dictate whether subsidies will be increased or decreased, but only in fractions. Washington will continue to provide many billions of dollars to promote, support, and perhaps even rescue private enterprises. Subsidies are here to stay.

Since that is the case, it is important to have a clear plan for the future. The world's economy is changing so fast, its resources shifting so drastically, and the needs of its people becoming so great that haphazard programs will not work. Government subsidies and public policy in general must be, above all else, practical, fair, and responsible in purpose.

[87]

For Further Reading

A number of sources may be useful in wading through the vast subject of government subsidies and what they mean. Publications by the U.S. government are a good place to start. *The United States Government Manual* (Washington, DC: U.S. Government Printing Office, Annually) provides a detailed breakdown of the branches, departments, agencies, offices, and programs of the federal government. *The Budget of the United States Government* and its accompanying booklet *Special Analyses* list and describe some of the major subsidy expenditures. Statements of principle and purpose introduce sections on agriculture, transportation, energy, and others. Both publications are available in government depository libraries and U.S. Government Printing Office bookstores throughout the country.

Basic economics textbooks are useful in understanding the basic operation, underlying theory, and implications of specific programs and the subsidized economy in general. The classic is Paul Samuelson's *Economics* (11th ed., New York: McGraw-Hill, 1980). Lloyd G. Reynolds' *Econom-

ics: A General Introduction (4th ed., Homewood, IL: Richard D. Irwin, 1973) also gives good coverage, especially of farm policy and price supports. A more sophisticated analysis of subsidies can be found in *Public Policies Toward Business,* by William G. Shepherd and Clair Wilcox (6th ed., Homewood, IL: Richard D. Irwin, 1979).

General insights, opinions, and recommendations on the relations between the government and private sector are thoughtfully and clearly presented in Ronald Miller's *Revitalizing America: Politics for Prosperity* (New York: Simon and Schuster, 1982); Murray Weidenbaum's *Business, Government, and the Public* (2nd ed., Englewood Cliffs, NJ: Prentice-Hall, 1981) and other of his works; and the reports of the President's Commission for a National Agenda for the Eighties, especially the "Report of the Panel on the American Economy" (Washington, DC, 1980).

The ongoing developments and controversies are perhaps best followed in such periodicals as *Business Week, Dun's Review, Congressional Quarterly Weekly Reports,* and the major news weeklies, as well as the daily newspaper.

Index

Defense: budget, 45–47; and Chrysler, 16; subsidies, 43–44, 45, 47–48
Depletion allowance, 41–42
Depression, the Great, 3, 10, 31–33, 36, 73, 87

Education as a subsidy, 43
Employment, 4, 7, 8, 11–12, 13–15
EPA (Environmental Protection Agency), 75

Farm: income stabilization, 49–51; subsidies, 45, 48–53, 64–65, 66; surplus, 51, 65. *See also* Agriculture; Farmers
Farmers: cash payments to, 40; problems of, 49–50
FCC (Federal Communications Commission), 74–75
FDA (Food and Drug Administration), 53
Foreign-trade development, 43
Free-market capitalism, 5, 63, 66–71; principles of, 23–24, 67. *See also* Mixed economy
FTC (Federal Trade Commission), 74; vs. lobbies, 77–79
Full Employment Act, 36, 37

General Motors Corporation, 9–10, 21
Germany, West, 85–86
Government control, 21–24, 71, 82; expansion of, 21–22, 28, 66–67, *see also* Subsidies, history of; vs. free-market theory, 23–26, 63, 66–71. *See also* Mixed economy; Regulation
Great Society, 37
Greenspan, Alan, 15

Highways, 54, 60
Hoover, Herbert, 33

Housing construction, 37, 41, 64
Human welfare, 22, 25, 36–37, 57–59, 63, 74

Iacocca, Lee A., 19
Industry (U.S.): decline in, 81–83; unified plan for, 83–87
ITT (International Telephone and Telegraph Company), 79

Jackson, Andrew, 27
Japan: auto industry in, 10–11; industrial planning, 85–86, 87; management, 81
Johnson, Lyndon B., 37

Kennedy, Edward, 87
Kennedy, John F., 37
King, Coretta Scott, 57–59, 63

Loan guarantees, 40–41, 55; in bailouts, 7, 17–20, 38
Loans, 40–41, 50, 55
Lobbying, 19, 72–73, 76–80, 82
Lockheed Aircraft Corporation, 38, 62, 84
Long, Russell B., 13

Mass transit, 54, 55, 63
Miller, William G., 7, 17, 19
Mixed economy, 27–38, 67; history of, 29–38; and planning, 83–84; and teamwork, 84–87

Nader, Ralph, 15, 77
National Agenda, Commission for, 61–62, 83, 86–87
National Industrial Recovery Act, 31–33
New Deal, 31–34, 48
New Frontier, 37
Nixon administration, 38, 79
NRA (National Recovery Administration), 33

[91]

Oil industry, 41–42, 63, 79
OPEC (Organization of Petroleum Exporting Countries), 10
OSHA (Occupational Safety and Health Administration), 75

Penn Central Railroad, 37–38, 62, 83
Postal Service, U.S., 29, 42
Price supports, 50–52, 64–65, 66
Proxmire, William, 15
PWA (Public Works Administration), 33

Railroads, 27–28, 29, 30–31, 54, 55. *See also* Penn Central
Rationing, 34
Reagan, Ronald, 20; and budget cuts, 3, 22, 24, 45–47, 51–53, 55–56; vs. government control, 22–24, 71, 76, 82; vs. lobbies, 80
Reconstruction Finance Corporation (RFC), 33, 34, 87
Regulation by government, 22, 72–76; and Chrysler, 16–17; cost of, 75–76; functions of, 74–75; and lobbying, 73
Research and development, 43, 47–48; as subsidy, 61, 82
Reuss, Henry, 87
Riccardo, John J., 1–3, 7, 8, 13, 16–17, 17–19
Roosevelt, Franklin D., 31–33, 48

Samuelson, Paul A., 29, 31, 88
Services as subsidies, 42–43
Shipbuilding, 35, 40, 55, 86
Small Business Administration, 61, 64
Smith, Adam, 23, 28, 66, 69
Special interest groups. *See* Lobbying
Stockman, David, 24, 51–52

Subsidies: categorized, 39–44; vs. free-market theory, 23–26, 62–63; future of, 87; history of, 27–38; indirect, 43–44; to individual companies, 37–38, *see also* Chrysler; measuring effectiveness of, 42, 43; purposes of, 4–5, 35–37, 45–46, 48; and Reagan cuts, 3, 22–23, 82–83; scope of, 3, 4–5. *See also* Subsidy; Subsidy system
Subsidy, defined, 3–4
Subsidy system: confusion in, 62, 83–84; evaluated, 59–60, 61–66; inequities in, 5, 57–59, 63; objectives of, 59, 60–66; and a unified plan, 83–84
Supply in free-market theory, 67–69
Surplus (government) as subsidy, 43

Tariffs as subsidies, 43
Tax benefits, 41–42
Taxpayers, 5, 63–64, 65
Technology, 60, 70, 81, 82
Transportation, 45, 53–56, 60
TVA (Tennessee Valley Authority), 33

U.S. Maritime Commission, 35
U.S. Treasury Department, 16, 17, 19

Van Buren, Martin, 27–28

War Finance Corporation, 30, 33
Wealth of Nations, The, 23
Wilson, Woodrow, 30–31, 33
World War I, 30–31, 73
World War II, 33, 34–35, 73, 87
WPA (Works Progress Administration), 33